Ethics in an Age of Savage Inequalities

Ethics in an Age of Savage Inequalities

James J. Winchester

LEXINGTON BOOKS
Lanham • Boulder • New York • London

Published by Lexington Books
An imprint of The Rowman & Littlefield Publishing Group, Inc.
4501 Forbes Boulevard, Suite 200, Lanham, Maryland 20706
www.rowman.com

Unit A, Whitacre Mews, 26-34 Stannary Street, London SE11 4AB

British Library Cataloguing in Publication Information Available

Library of Congress Cataloging-in-Publication Data

Winchester, James J.
Ethics in an age of savage inequalities / James J. Winchester.
pages cm.
Includes bibliographical references and index.
ISBN 978-1-4985-0448-5 (cloth : alk. paper) -- ISBN 978-1-4985-0450-8 (pbk. : alk. paper)
1. Ethics. 2. Social ethics. 3. Equality. I. Title.
BJ1012.W564 2015
170--dc23
                                        2015023825

∞ ™ The paper used in this publication meets the minimum requirements of American
National Standard for Information Sciences Permanence of Paper for Printed Library
Materials, ANSI/NISO Z39.48-1992.

Printed in the United States of America

To Adrian, Sophie, Sunita, the man who gave me the figs, and the woman who gave me half her bread as well as all those who I have met who opened their hearts to me.

Contents

Acknowledgments

As a middle-class person from the United States I have had the opportunity to travel across many parts of the globe and meet many different people. Once while hitchhiking along the then sparsely inhabited Mediterranean coastal road of northern Morocco, I got stuck. I waited for six hours and only two cars went by—both headed in the opposite direction. At some point during the afternoon, an old man wandered by on foot. He stopped and spoke to me briefly, but I could not understand his language—it was probably Tamazight (often called Berber). In an act of kindness, he reached into his pocket and gave me a few delicious purple figs and then went on his way. Throughout the two months I spend hitchhiking around Morocco, I experienced innumerable acts of kindness from many people of very modest means. Another time, also along the sparsely populated northern coast of Morocco, a woman dressed in black and driving animals in front of her came up to me, reached under her dress, took out a loaf of freshly baked home-made bread, broke it, and gave me half. These were not my first or last experiences of the generosity of those with modest means, but those acts of kindness—and many others—have stuck with me. Remembering those acts is part of what motivates me to want to think about how I can give back to strangers who are not as fortunate as I.

I want to acknowledge and thank my mother and my father who taught me from a very early age that it was important to think about others and that our circle of concern should include all human beings. My brother Robert and sister Julie cared for me—their little brother—even if at times they wondered why their parents did not stop at two children. Dennis, Amma, Sabi, and Brad have adopted me and cared for me as if I were a blood relative as have Lou, Barb, Larry, Sarah, Emma, Tim, Mary, Michael, Oscar, Julie, and Howie. I truly appreciate the continued care and affection of this large extended family. I have friends all over the world who opened up their hearts and their worlds to me. They cared for me and taught me and I truly appreciate all they have given. I appreciate the ways that teachers, students and colleagues have supported the writing of this book. Among the colleagues who have nurtured my intellectual life at Georgia College are JJ Arias, Warner Belanger, Kelli Brown, Mark Causey, Steve Dorman, Funke Fontenot, Ralph France, Carlos Herrera, Sabrina Hom, Sid Littlefield, Mary Magoulick, Sunita Manian, Jim McManmon, Stephanie Opperman, Ken Procter, John Sallstrom, Jameliah Shorter, Costas Spirou, Charles Ubah, Huaiyu Wang, Bob Wilson, and Veronica Womack. Others who have read and given valuable feedback on this book include Nuru Akinyemi, Robert Bernasconi, Christophe Bonazzi, Gilles Bonazzi, David Carr, Robert Davis, Gene McCreary, Fabio Morales, Robert Reich, Louis Ruprecht and Cynthia Willett. Among the many current and former students who have pushed me to think about philosophical issues are Mina Adams, Tiras Barrett, Maria Bermudez, Chloe Bowman, Zach Brown, James Callahan, Won Choe, Jennifer Clark, Courtney Conrad, Jordan Cook, Zach Disher, Chris Eby, Matthew Gilbo, Thomas Giordano, Graham Gordon, Kafia Haile, Susan Heikkela, Brandi Iryrshe, Brittany Johnson, Dylan Jones, Rachel Kahn, Thomas Keefe, Justin Markowitz, Robert McDaniel, Hannah Miller, Austin Moore, Abby O'Callaghan, Emma Nestor, Hunter Patrick, Aimee Petitt, Ben Racz, Elizabeth Rainwater, Brandon Romanos, Kelsey Stone, Charles Spencer, Brent Tripp, and Sierra Watkins. I also appreciate and would like to thank the fine editors at Lexington, Jana Hodges-Kluck, Natalie Mandziuk, and Kari Waters, for their great work and support. I owe the greatest debt to Sunita, who not only believed in this project, and enthusiastically supported it and strengthened my arguments through countless discussions, but also taught me most of what I know about the economic realities behind these problems. I give thanks to all of these as well as those I have forgotten.

I want to thank Georgia College for having given me a funded research leave. I appreciate David Jones who arranged for me to give a lecture on this topic at Kennesaw State University and John Duffield's invitation to Sunita Manian and myself to give a lecture on these topics at Georgia State University. I want to thank Prafulla Car and the Forum on Contemporary Theory where I have presented several papers related to this project. I also want to thank the Association of Third World Studies where I have also presented a number of papers that were reworked and incorporated into this book. Finally, I would like to thank those who will take the time to read this book and contribute to the project of figuring out how to live in this time when many have a great deal and many do not.

All the proceeds that would have gone to the author will be donated directly to GiveWell, an organization discussed in this work which is dedicated to evaluating and improving upon the effectiveness of charitable organizations.

Introduction

Of Wealth and Ethical Responsibility

Even in these hard economic times, I am, relatively speaking, wealthy and am writing this book to invite other relatively wealthy people like myself to reflect on their ethical responsibilities in this world of savage inequalities. Before you assume you are not relatively wealthy, read a few more sentences. When claiming to be relatively wealthy I am comparing myself to the more than 1 billion people in the world, who live on less than $1.25 a day and the 2.5 billion (together these 3.5 billion people are almost one-half of the world's population) who live on less than $2.00 a day. Are you thinking that a dollar might go further in the parts of the world where most of these people live? The World Bank, which compiles these statistics, has already taken this fact into account. When calculating the earnings of people, the World Bank measures how much people can purchase with their earnings in their home country. So when it says that someone is living on a dollar a day it means that these people can buy in their home country what a dollar would buy in the United States. To buy a four dollar Happy Meal in their own country, someone earning a dollar a day would have to work for four days. Given the exchange rates between poor countries and wealthy ones, if third world workers try to convert their earnings into U.S. dollars they would usually get something like twenty-five cents on the dollar. For those making a dollar a day, it would take sixteen days to accumulate enough of their own local currency to get four U.S. dollars and buy the Happy Meal in the United States. Wealth is a relative thing. Compared to Bill Gates, I am not wealthy. Compared to almost half the world I—underpaid philosophy professor that I am—am very wealthy indeed. And even in these uncertain times, there are literally hundreds of millions of people like me. [1]

I call these inequalities "savage" (a phrase borrowed from Jonathan Kozol's book about poverty in the United States which I will discuss) because
there are many who are dying or leading short and truly miserable lives while
many of us are living lives with many luxuries. Those making less than a
dollar a day are living in what the World Bank has labeled "absolute poverty." Their lives are made miserable by malnutrition, illiteracy, disease, squal-
id living conditions, high infant mortality rates and low life expectancy. They
often lack the most basic of human needs—not just food, but clean drinking
water, access to bathrooms, roofs over their heads, and even shoes. I own a
car and live in an apartment with electricity, refrigeration, air conditioning
and two bathrooms. Even in this time of economic uncertainty, I can afford
to go out to restaurants. Compared to the majority of the world, I am a very
wealthy man. Some inequality can be helpful or at least not harmful to the
world. The current inequality is "savage" because, for among other reasons,
many are dying from poverty while others live with an obscene amount of
luxury. As we will see, even middle-class life is often purchased at the
expense of the poor.

The poor in the United States are often not as poor as those living in
absolute poverty, but there are many people in the United States who are at
risk of going hungry. Thirty-four percent of African American children in the
United States live below the poverty line, according to government figures.[2]
And there are some people in the United States who are living on less than
$2.00 a day: 1.17 million children, according to a recent study.[3] Compared to
many people in the United States I am wealthy. I don't worry about not
having enough to eat, but, like many others, I am at risk because I eat too
much. Many who have written about global poverty and ethical responsibility have done so without addressing inequality within wealthy nations. The
poor in the United States, for example, usually have food and a roof over
their head. Many have televisions and air conditioning, but often they do not
have access to good health care. There probably is a connection between the
fact that the United States has the greatest inequality of any wealthy nation
and the fact that the United States gives the least foreign aid, as a percentage
of GNP, of any wealthy nation. Having learned to look past the poor in our
midst, we look past the distant poor as well. This book attempts to help
relatively wealthy people think about our responsibilities to the poor. What
are the responsibilities of the relatively wealthy to those living in absolute
poverty and what do the relatively wealthy owe to those living in poverty in
the United States?

Some who agree with me that the world is indeed marked by savage
inequalities might ask if an ethical treatise aimed at the relatively wealthy is
naïve? It is easy to see that there are savage inequalities in this world, but
isn't it naïve to think anything less than a radical change to the world's
economic order is required? Precisely because I am not wealthy compared to

Bill Gates, instead of focusing on what individuals should do, I should think about how the world should change. Slavoj Zizek might call my proposals "the drivel of a left-liberal moron." He argues that capitalism always escapes from attempts to reform it and nothing less than revolution will change things.[4] Unlike Jonathan Swift, I truly believe in modest proposals. I would like to contribute to changing the world, not just interpreting it, but I think we are more likely to change the world through persuasion rather than revolution. Like many I have lost faith in the otherworldly rewards promised to saints and am seeking rewards in this world. This is not an entirely bad thing. So many of the great "crusades"—those of the Middle Ages and those of the right and the left in our own time—seem now to be ill-conceived, wasted sacrifices at best, and at worst they are poorly disguised attempts at imperial conquest. Many lives have been wasted in the service of crusades, not to mention the loss of life among the "infidels." Systemic changes are needed. I will be arguing that we should make modest steps as individuals. We can as individuals give money (although, as we will see in chapter 1, there are reasons not to call our giving charity) and work to reduce our environmental impact even while we work for broader systemic changes. We should work both within and across national borders in principled coalitions with others to change the global economic systems that unduly harm the poor. In so doing, we will probably help ourselves as well. By not asking too much, one can make a stronger case for taking these actions.

This project draws on the work of both those who encourage individual action and those who favor systemic action. Peter Singer, for example, focuses on what we as individuals should do and asks us to give money. I admire his work a great deal. He has been writing about world poverty since the early 1970s and has done more to bring attention to the ethical implications of global poverty, and for that matter many other important ethical issues, than any other philosopher. In *The Life You Can Save: Acting Now to End World Poverty* he suggests a sliding scale and asks those of us making less than $100,000 to donate 1 percent of our earnings to charities that are devoted to ending the worst international poverty. He estimates that if the super wealthy gave a moderate amount and those of us who earn less gave a very moderate amount, we would be able to generate more than enough money to rid the world of absolute poverty.

Singer regales us with tales of the super wealthy. Paul Allen had the good fortune to grow up with Bill Gates and work with him for a short period of time, and the good sense to hold on to his Microsoft stock. He is now one of the richest men in the world and has among his play toys three "monster yachts." One of them was, at the time of its construction, the world's largest, costing more than $200 million to build and $20 million a year to maintain. It is not only, however, in first world nations that we find wealthy, extravagant people. Singer does not discuss Mukesh Ambani, who was fortunate to have

a father who was born poor but then created the world's largest textile producer, Reliance Industries. Mukesh Ambani has recently built his family of
five (himself, his wife and three children) a twenty-seven story tower in
Mumbai. It has, among other amenities, three helipads, hanging gardens, and
six floors of parking. Some have estimated that this "house" cost $1 billion to
build. It does not take a subtle philosophical argument to suggest that these
super rich have an ethical obligation to do something to help those who have
no roof over their heads or access to clean water. But this book is for those of
us who do not have such wealth. It is true that given how much even the
moderately wealthy have, it seems that those of us who have disposable
income should give money to charitable organizations to relieve poverty, but
we may wonder whether the money we give will do any good. One hears of
fraudulent aid organizations and even if organizations are well-intentioned,
questions often remain how effective they are. Lack of corruption does not
insure efficiency. Social programs and charitable organizations are as subject
to failure as any other human endeavor. There is no point in giving simply to
assuage a bad conscience. I will examine these objections that are often
raised about charitable giving and will also examine how much we should
give.

Unlike Singer, Thomas Pogge emphasizes the need to help change the
systems that unduly disadvantage the poor. Even a cursory glance at the
current world order lends considerable credence to Pogge's claim that there
is much that is unjust. First, mineral wealth may be the most telling example
of the problems with the current world order for it rarely benefits and usually
harms the people who live on top of it. Many of the world's poor are suffering because of their proximity to mineral wealth. As we will see, middle-
class people throughout the world—as well as the owners of yachts—who
drive cars and heat and cool their homes, or for that matter use cell phones,
profit from the exploitation of these people.

A second systemic problem that needs to be fixed is the unfair structuring
of world trade. Most experts agree that previous trade agreements have not
helped poor countries. The Doha Round of trade negotiations was supposed
to remedy this. These negotiations once again faltered over agricultural policies. India, a democracy where poor farmers are a large and crucial voting
bloc, wanted the right to limit imports of food in order to protect its vulnerable farmers. Subsidies and protective schemes benefit powerful northern
agricultural corporations at the expense of third world farmers. Brazil and
other third world exporters of food wanted the United States and Europe to
cut back on their agricultural subsides. Given how many of the world's
poorest people are subsistence farmers, agricultural policy is extremely important to many of the world's most vulnerable people.

A third problem in the current world order is the exploitation of workers.
Many of the world's poor are laboring in factories in the third world to

produce the things we use every day, while others are threatened by our energy-intensive lifestyles. As hard as these factory jobs usually are, they are also often, but not always, better than working on the farm. Nevertheless, all workers should be afforded basic rights and a living wage. Even within the United States there are many laboring to make my lifestyle possible—clerks in discount stores, dishwashers in restaurants, adjuncts teaching in universities, to name just three—who are not making living-wages.

Finally, there is the problem of pollution. The lifestyle of even the middle class in the United States is contributing to global warming. This is a dangerous trend for the global poor, in particular for poor farmers who lack irrigation and rely on rains. My use of the environment is also creating serious problems for those who will, hopefully, follow us on this earth. Owning a car is something that relatively few of the world's people can afford. There is strong evidence that the greenhouse gases that cars produce are causing sea levels to rise. Rising sea levels threaten hundreds of millions of people who live in low-lying areas in, among other places, Bangladesh, China, and Egypt, or, for that matter, Florida. It also threatens small indigenous groups living on low-lying islands and the Arctic Circle. The obligation to act to end poverty becomes stronger when we realize the way that the wealth of even the middle class is purchased through the exploitation of the poor and vulnerable. As one of the relatively wealthy, what, if anything, can I do about this?

Singer's and Pogge's concern with global poverty is not universal among philosophers. One of the most popular philosophical books on justice in recent memory is Michael Sandel's *Justice: What's the Right Thing to Do?* Sandel is often labeled a communitarian, which implies that he believes there are very few universally held notions of justice, but justice is defined relative to a particular culture. Sandel does not call himself a communitarian, but his works are full of references to the importance of communities in determining justice. Communitarian or not, Sandel engages in this book, and in his Harvard course on which this book is based—apparently one of the most popular courses ever offered at Harvard—in a discussion almost entirely about justice in the United States. Sandel ends his book with a poignant warning about the gap between rich and poor *in the United States*. He warns that this inequality undermines "the solidarity that democratic citizenship requires."[5] The rich in the United States are retreating from public schools and public transportation, and consequently public services are deteriorating. Solidarity becomes hard to cultivate when the rich and poor lead totally separate lives.

How many of the goods and services that we consume in the United States are produced or sold by people who are not receiving a living wage? There will always be questions about exactly what constitutes a living wage and whether or not companies can afford to give everyone a living wage. But the principle that those who supply us with goods and services should earn enough to provide themselves and their families with food, lodging, health care, and leisure time is unproblematic. Again, discerning the act that should follow from the principle is not always easy. For example, how often do we in the United States eat in a restaurant where the people who cook for us and clean up after us do not receive health insurance? Does this mean that we should boycott such restaurants? Should we lobby the government to supply health care and affordable housing to those who earn wages too low to afford these basic necessities? How many of the people who provide child care, mow lawns, do janitorial work, or build apartments, houses and office spaces do not receive a living wage? Should we refuse to buy goods and services from stores that do not, in our view, pay living wages? Should we patronize such stores, but attempt to change them? Should the problems be addressed by raising wages or by the government providing more services to the working poor? It is impossible to say in advance how we should act in each situation. Problems are easier to find than to solve. In the case of poverty, enunciating the ethical principles is the easier part. Applying them is more difficult. As we will see, ethical issues demand we look at the particular features of each situation.

In the United States the wealthy often look past the poor in our midst. One does not have to live in a gated community to erect sophisticated barriers to hide the plight of those who clean the stores where we shop; harvest our food; cook our food and then wash our dishes; sell us our consumer goods; and build our homes and places of work. But it is striking how Sandel can write so eloquently about inequality in the United States and rarely address global inequality. In his book we almost never hear about the travails of the many people who labor in countries outside of the United States. The lives of those living in the United States are made possible by laborers in the United States, but also by laborers who live on the other side of the world. Energy-intensive lifestyles affect people the world over. The world is simply too interconnected to stop debates about justice at the border of a nation-state. I don't know of a moral philosopher from any culture who says that one is free to disregard the effect of one's actions on others if that other lives on the other side of a national border. This book seeks to make visible the global and the local underpinnings of even middle-class lives and help us think about what we owe these people. Questions about means are legitimate, but it is unethical to ignore the conditions of those who labor or suffer so that we might lead our middle-class lives. We will also think about our obligations to those who are desperately poor, but not directly affected by our lives.

A contrast is often drawn between Sandel and John Rawls, another Harvard philosopher and very possibly the most famous political philosopher of the twentieth century. Whereas Sandel is skeptical about our ability to define justice universally, Rawls formulated a theory of justice that he believed was in some sense a universal ideal, but at the same time he left it up to individual societies or, to use the word from the title of one his last works, "peoples" to come together to define justice. Both men build their theories of justice thinking very little about the world outside the United States. Sandel doubts whether people from different societies can agree on what constitutes the good life and therefore he doubts our ability to form notions of justice that transcend cultures. Suppose for a moment that Sandel is right and it is impossible to define the just outside the bounds of a particular community. Who exactly is our community? The distant needy are really not so distant and those who live in relative proximity are often not acting very neighborly. Who is my brother? The investment banker whose risky practices brought the world economy to the brink of collapse? I suspect that even though I am of the same generation, and share the same language and nationality with many investment bankers, I might have a very different take on the justice of their acts. Are the oil company executives my brothers? On the one hand, they are out scouring the world for oil so that I might drive my car, but the oil spill in the Gulf of Mexico has brought home to the United States what the people of the Niger Delta, to cite only one example among many, have known for more than forty years. Large multinational oil companies will, when given the chance, cut corners, and the people living on top of the oil as well as the entire country suffer enormously. The Niger Delta, like many of the oil-producing regions of the world, has been devastated by the extraction of oil that has gone into fueling our cars, and the Nigerian government has been corrupted by these oil revenues as well. All of Nigeria has been cursed by this "sweet light crude" that is so easy to refine, ship to the United States and put in our cars. According to the CIA's *World Factbook*, Nigeria ranks third in the world in GNP (180th in GDP per capita PPP) and 212th out of 223 in life expectancy. Do I not owe something to the people of Nigeria?

There are ten million farmers in West Africa who would like to grow the cotton for my shirts. They would do it without subsidies and in a much more environmentally sustainable way than is done in West Texas. Who is my brother? The wealthy farmer who receives subsidies from the U.S. government or the West African farmer who works long days trying to provide for his or her family and who would willingly produce cotton in a more ecologically sound way without taking a subsidy from my tax dollars? As the world becomes increasingly dominated by large multinational corporations, the well-being of the vast majority of the industrialized world and the nonindustrialized world will rely on building principled coalitions between distant peoples. We should work to change the economic systems that exploit the world's poor. In particular, we should address the ways that the extraction of minerals, the global trade system, and global warming are oppressing the poor. And in working to end the exploitation of the poor we may very well end up benefitting ourselves as well. One learns a great deal by observing how the powerful act when they think no one is watching. We need to tame the beasts—the large multinational corporations that make our lives possible, often at great cost to the vulnerable.

Unlike his Harvard colleague Sandel, Amartya Sen argues that debates about justice benefit from a variety of global perspectives and warns against the parochialism that accompanies discussions that take place within the confines of one nation. Like Sandel, Sen rejects the notion that reason can formulate an ideal transcendental universal theory of justice, but Sen does think that there are some things that are so obviously unjust that reasonable people from different cultures will see them as unjust. Sen suggests we employ Adam Smith's notion of the impartial spectator to help us formulate an idea of what is just. Without being able to formulate a precise ideal theory of justice (as Rawls tried to do), Sen argues that we can see that an impartial spectator would recognize that some things are obviously unjust. Considering the perspectives of others, including those who live in other countries, can help us avoid parochialism and achieve at least a limited degree of impartiality. He suggests that discussions of women's rights, the use of torture and the death penalty are three cases where global discussions can lead to a "fuller assessment" that overcomes local prejudices. Sen also argues that our discussions of justice should be international because what happens in one country often has huge consequences for the rest of the world.[6] As an example, Sen cites the United States' invasion of Iraq. It is indeed striking that Sandel can publish a major work on justice in 2009, a work which is the culmination of many years of teaching at one of the leading educational institutions in the United States and a work that has achieved an unparalleled level of public recognition, and not address the justice of the Iraq war. We can learn a great deal from Sandel's discussion of inequality in the United States, but his failure to engage the ethics of the United States' invasion of Iraq stands as a stunning testimony to Sandel's insularity and raises questions about the insularity of the Harvard undergraduates who flock to his course. We live in a world that is much too interconnected to restrict our discussions of ethics and justice to one country. The United States, in particular, is a bull in this fragile world. Given the number of Iraqis who died because of the invasion and the millions more who were forced into exile, surely the Iraq war, as Sen argues, was unjust for a number of reasons. We do not have to know exactly what justice is to say that it was unjust. Even apart from the invasion of Iraq, as a middle-class person who owns a car and uses air conditioning, part of that bull's damage is done to support my life style. As much as I admire Sen's commitment to global justice, and agree with him that the Iraq war was obviously unjust, many dispute this claim. How can we know who is truly being impartial? What do we say to those who stubbornly refuse to see as we stubbornly believe an impartial spectator would see? In chapter 1, I will address these questions and suggest how we might modify the notion of the impartial spectator in light of these problems.

At least since Aristotle, many philosophers have concluded that ethics is more of an art than a science. As much as we might want to be certain that we are acting ethically, each situation is different. Even if our intentions are just, we can never be certain about the outcome of our actions. Aristotle maintains, and I agree, that the first principles of ethics are not scientifically demonstrable. Both ends and means must be arrived at through a process of deliberation. Prudence is required and that is why ethical deliberation requires maturity whereas mathematics does not. Lack of certainty should not paralyze us, but it should inspire humility. Aristotle also warns us about the power of pleasure to distort our thinking. In trying to be ethical, he writes that we should react to pleasure as the wise men reacted to Helen of Troy—send her away lest you err! How sad that our temptations—oversized houses, luxury cars and other material goods—are so banal compared to the face that launched a thousand ships.

Aristophanes, the great comic poet, once portrayed Socrates swinging from the rafters of a building, philosophizing about the ass of a flea—lost in the clouds of theory. He was surely not the first or the last to accuse philosophers of having their heads in the clouds. Like all great comedy, the depiction contains much truth. The charge that philosophers have their heads in the clouds is a specter that really should haunt all attempts at ethical theory, but philosophers are not the only ones with their heads in the clouds. Many turn their backs on the poor. One of my goals is to turn our gaze back to the poor in the United States as well as the poor abroad. I want to explore the stories behind the extraction of minerals and rare earth metals. I will also look at stories of sweatshop workers and African farmers as well as stories of the poor in the United States. The goal of this book is not to impart the truth, but to help make the lives of those who are suffering to support even middle-class lives more visible. I want to engender discussion in the hope of dissipating some of the clouds that surround our discussions of poverty. We live in a world of unparalleled wealth. We may, for the first time in human history, be able to reduce or even rid the world of its worst poverty. If this book is able to clear away some of the clouds surrounding the savage inequalities of our day, perhaps it will motivate its readers to act and will give some guidance on how to act so that all people might have access to food, clothing, shelter, health care and leisure time for themselves and their families.

To be more precise, chapter 1 "Cobbling Together an Ethics" begins with Aristotle's insight that ethics is an imprecise endeavor. Recognizing that every situation is different, I argue with Aristotle that prudently judging the particular situation and the action that should follow is the key to understanding our ethical responsibilities in our savagely unequal world. Prudence does carry the risk of simply embracing the perceived wisdom—as Aristotle's misogyny and countenance of slavery attests, but, at its best, ethical theory prudently shakes the perceived wisdom. I also discuss Nietzsche's claim that morality often seduces and deludes us. Aware of how wrong ethical theories can go, I argue that philosophy should not just interpret the world, but change it. The chapter ends with a discussion of the work of some of the most important writers on global inequality, including Peter Singer, Thomas Pogge and Amartya Sen. I have learned a great deal from all of them as well as others. In particular, using Sen's insight, I discuss how we can recognize obvious wrongs even if we do not have a perfectly formed system of justice. Once we become aware of the savage inequalities of our day, we can use the resources of several thinkers to cobble together an ethics.

Chapter 2 "The Luck of Our Draw" challenges the notion that wealth and poverty are largely the result of personal initiative. Too much of our fate is determined by the accident of our birth, i.e., the luck of our draw. Charity is not the primary answer to the ethical issues surrounding poverty, but given the role that chance plays in our accumulation of wealth, it is incumbent upon those of us who have disposable wealth to make charitable contributions to aid the poor.

Starting with our use of minerals, chapter 3 "Minerals, International Trade, Fair Trade, and Living Wages" traces out some of the ways that middle-class lives are made possible by the exploitation of the poor. From the exploitation surrounding the extraction of oil to the rules of international trade, there are many ways that middle-class people benefit at the poor's expense. These people are owed restitution and not charity. In addition, some of the poor are laboring to make middle-class lives possible, both in the United States and abroad. We owe those who labor on our behalf a living wage. There are legitimate debates about how to go about ensuring a living wage for all workers, but once we see the many ways in which we are unduly privileged by the current world order, the ethical imperative to change the current structure becomes hard to deny. I suggest that fair trade offers one possible vehicle to help address the savage inequalities of our time.

Chapter 4 "Environmental Justice" looks at the ways that the poor often pay for the pollution of the rich. To give one example, the erratic weather trends brought on by global warming affect poor farmers who rely on rainfall. Rising sea waters are threatening many of the world's poor in Bangladesh, China, and Egypt. Given the lack of public transportation in the United States, many of us have become dependent on our cars. As the people in China, India, and other parts of the developing world begin to buy cars, refrigerators and air conditioners, the problem threatens to become much worse. Changing our lifestyle to reduce global warming may be one of the most challenging ethical tests that middle-class people face.

In the conclusion "The Way Forward" I admit that the problems are daunting, but argue that we can and should act. We can take small steps even while we work to make the larger systemic changes to make the world more just. It is important to join with the poor to make these systemic changes. As we work to reform global economic systems, we should give money to alleviate poverty, support initiatives such as fair trade and reduce our carbon footprint.

NOTES

1. If you want to calculate where you are on the world's income scale more precisely see Branko Milanovic, "Where in the Global Income Distribution are You?" in *The Have and Have-Nots: A Brief and Idiosyncratic History of Global Inequality* (New York: Basic, 2011). To condense his findings he argues that those individuals who make more than $34,000 in the United States (after taxes) are in the world's top 1 percent.

2. http://pubdb3.census.gov/macro/032004/pov/new01_100_06.htm

3. H. Luke Shaefer and Kathryn Edin, "Rising Extreme Poverty in the United States and the Response of Federal Means-Tested Programs" National Poverty Center Working Paper Series #13 – 06 May 2013 cited in an opinion piece by Thomas P. Edsall *New York Times* 6/17/2014.

4. Slavoj Zizek, *The Year of Dreaming Dangerously* (London: Verso, 2012), 15.

5. Michael Sandel, *Justice: What's the Right Thing to Do?* (New York: Farrar, Straus and Giroux), 266.

6. Sen, *The Idea of Justice*, (Cambridge: Harvard University Press, 2009), 71.

Chapter One

Cobbling Together an Ethics

"Philosophers have only interpreted the world, in various ways: the point, however, is to change it."

—Karl Marx "Theses on Feuerbach, XI"[1]

Many philosophers, particularly in the last 200 years, have grown suspicious of ethics as well as philosophy's ability to define the just society. More than 2,000 years of debate in the West has not produced consensus about many very basic questions regarding ethics of individual acts and the justice of larger social arrangements. There are lively debates about these issues in non-Western traditions as well. Philosophers disagree sharply about ethical paradigms and principles of justice. There are at least three major ethical paradigms in the contemporary Western philosophical tradition: utilitarianism, deontological or duty-based ethics, and virtue ethics. Within each of these schools there are disagreements. And there are a large number of philosophers who argue that ethics is, at worst, a guise for self-interested acts and, at best, hopelessly naive. Similarly, there are communitarians, liberals, libertarians, and others disagreeing about what constitutes a just society. If after literally thousands of years of ethical reflection and reflection on justice there is little that is not in dispute, what hope might we have that philosophical reflection can help us decide what we as individuals should do about the savage inequalities of our day or what a just society might be? Philosophers rarely promise certainty and indeed I would warn against those who would, but our lack of definitive answers does not mean that philosophical reflection has nothing to offer our attempts to create a more just world.[2]

PRUDENCE

Aristotle offers a particularly insightful model for dealing with the uncertainty that surrounds ethical deliberations, but his writings are not without their quirks. Among other things, he argues that some people are naturally ("from the hour of their birth") suited to be slaves while others are suited to rule.[3] In other words, slavery is not a violation of nature; it is necessary for the proper functioning of society because humans with slavish natures need masters. The slave has a very limited power of deliberation and therefore needs a master to direct him. Aristotle also argues that men are naturally superior to women. It is unclear what Aristotle thinks about female slaves—he "wastes" no time reflecting on their lives. Free women are said to be capable of deliberation, but they lack the ability to deliberate with authority.[4] Men are called upon to help them with that.

I called these views quirky and so they seem to most of us today, even if his views of women and slaves were widely, although not universally, shared in his time. At its worst, Aristotle's ethics is an apology for the status quo—taking its society's views on ethical issues to be correct. For example, he claims that happiness is the goal of political science because "both the many and the cultivated" agree that it is the goal.[5] Conventional wisdom is a tricky base upon which to build an ethical system. The views of "the many and the cultivated" often seem, with the benefit of hindsight, unduly popular and less than cultivated. Martin Luther King, Jr.'s *Why We Can't Wait*, to name but one famous example, was a direct challenge to the perceived wisdom of "the many and the cultivated" who felt the civil rights movement was moving too fast in demanding civil rights. I will be arguing that the many and the cultivated have become too easily reconciled with the profound poverty within our world and indeed within the United States. We have developed subtle and not so subtle coping skills that allow us to live, all too comfortably, alongside this poverty and profit from it.

That said, trying to shake the perceived wisdom is not without its risks. Grandiose visions of would-be saviors are often the stuff of comedy and, at times, have inspired terror. Marx sought to change the world and in his name Stalin and others murdered millions, but Marx also helped to inspire the international workers movements that raised the standard of living of workers, particularly in Europe. History is littered with good intentions gone tragically wrong. Philosophers devoted not just to interpreting the world, but changing it, must consider carefully the possible effects of their prescriptions, and at times conventional wisdom can be an effective antidote to the excesses of theoretical wisdom.

But back to Aristotle, the misogynist, classist, defender of slavery from whom I plan to take some ethical insights. To the problems with Aristotle's ethics already mentioned let me add one more. Aristotle's *Nicomachean*

Ethics is a seminal work in Western ethical theory, but this book, like most of the writings we have from Aristotle, is not a finished product. It is a series of notes most probably assembled by Aristotle scholars. It jumps from topic to topic and even some of the sentences are incomplete. There are good reasons to be suspicious of an ethical system based on lecture notes that embraces slavery and misogyny and is based on the murky ground of prudential reasoning, but still there is much to be learned from Aristotle's approach to ethics in general and from *Nicomachean Ethics* in particular.

Most importantly, as I have already mentioned, Aristotle appreciates the imprecise nature of ethics. Aristotle delineates between that which can be known with certainty and that which can be known only approximately and in outline. He argues that ethics deals with human actions and given that no two situations will ever be exactly the same, treatises about ethics will always be somewhat imprecise—as the subject matter demands. Three times at the beginning of *Nicomachean Ethics*, Aristotle warns that ethics is inexact.[6] Like geometry, ethics requires first principles, but the challenge of ethics is applying those principles to the particular situation. Unlike geometry there is no certainty about how best to judge the situation. Aristotle compares ethics to medicine and navigation.[7] In each case decisions are not based solely on knowledge of a craft or technique, but the ability to discern the nature of the particular situation. One must be a keen judge of the particular moment in order to know how to apply the principle.

Prudence (*phronesis*) is the name Aristotle gives to the ability to choose the ethical act appropriate for the situation. Prudence is required to know how to achieve the ethical end and it is also required in choosing the end. There can be no science of prudence because human actions "admit of being otherwise" and we do not deliberate about acts that cannot be otherwise.[8] There is no reason to deliberate about the proofs of mathematics. They are either right or wrong, but attempts to improve the lives of the poor, however well-intentioned, can go tragically awry. Prudence requires reason, but reason alone will not ensure a prudent outcome. Prudent people—Pericles is Aristotle's preferred example—keenly judge the situation so as to bring happiness to themselves and to those whom they govern. In short, ethics cannot be done in the abstract. Ethics demands a rigorous study of how the principles are put into action as well as an appreciation of the nuances of the particular situation.

Aristotle ended his life in exile from his adopted city. He left to ensure that the Athenians would not kill him, as they had Socrates, and famously commented that he did not want to give Athens the chance to "sin twice against philosophy." It is not only in the West that philosophers dedicated to improving social life have run into difficulty. Confucius held minor political offices and died believing that he had made little impact, and yet it is probably that no other thinker has influenced as many human beings. Lao-Tzu, so the tradition goes, died in the wilderness. Even if these ethical thinkers led difficult lives, their theories have brought great benefits. Regardless of the stories of how Lao-Tzu ended his life alone, the *Tao Te Ching's* anti-materialist message and its criticisms of militarism have not lost their relevance. Slavery has been largely, but not totally abolished after a long struggle in which the ideas of the Stoics and others played important roles. Gandhi's ideas not only helped to bring about the end of colonialism, but also served as an inspiration for Martin Luther King, Jr. and the civil rights movement in the United States.

Throughout history, many great ideas have gone terribly wrong when put into practice. Reason and the theories it engenders cannot provide the definitive justification to act in such a way as to reduce human suffering, nor can reason be the sole motivating force for ethical action. Reason cannot tell us exactly which social arrangements will bring about the just society. Acting prudently to relieve the suffering of the poor is also difficult because in addition to individual acts, we will have to seek the political transformation of society. Prudently discerning how society should be changed, and how to act so that society will change, is difficult. Reason cannot insure that actions will turn out as planned, but reason in conjunction with our feelings and the best of conventional wisdom may motivate and guide our actions so that we who have in superabundance act prudently to improve the appalling conditions under which so many on this planet live.

Putting an end to global poverty is obviously a very big undertaking, although, as we will see, the world has never been in a better position to address it than now. The study of ethics and the study of social justice will not be able to say exactly what our ethical or social responsibilities are, or exactly what will work, but it can guide us. Philosophical reflection can help us examine our lives and our societies, motivate us to act and give us guidance about how we should act.

Like Aristotle, Amartya Sen argues that there can never be a perfect systematic account of justice. Even if we were able to formulate a perfect system of justice in the abstract, it would not help us in comparing two concrete instances of imperfect justice in the real world. Sen uses the analogy that knowing that the Mona Lisa is the most perfect painting ever made would not help us in assessing the relative merits of a Picasso versus a Dali. The conceptual work that philosophers do can help us gain new insights on issues of ethical responsibility and social justice, but, as Aristotle and Sen recognize, the real world presents us with a great deal of ambiguity. It is not hard to see that there is something wrong with the inequalities of our present age. As we trace out in chapters 3 and 4 how our wealth is often purchased at great cost to others and how energy-intensive lifestyles are endangering others, the necessity to act will become, I hope, obvious. I do not need a perfect understanding of justice to see that some things are unjust. I may not be able to formulate exactly what my duties are to reform, but as we study the ways of the world we will see that there are some things that are obviously unjust and some things we clearly should be doing in an effort to make the world more just.

Like Aristotle, Sen also urges us to pay careful attention to outcomes. Something may seem just in theory, but if it does not produce outcomes that are just, we must revise the theory. If, for example, income inequality has dramatically increased in the United States since 1979 and social mobility has decreased, then we must ask what systemic changes need to be made so that people truly have the opportunity to succeed and are not condemned to their station in life by the accident of their birth. If the rules of international trade are such that the world's poor farmers are being forced to compete with subsidized food from the wealthy nations then we need to change these rules. We do not have to have a perfect understanding of justice to see that the current world trade rules are not treating the poor third world farmers justly. Philosophers have a strong affinity for abstract schemes. Abstract notions of justice can help us analyze real-world situations, but we must not fetishize abstract theory. Theory helps us recognize injustice, but it cannot give us an absolute standard for what is just nor tell us with absolute certainty how we should act.

Unlike Aristotle, Sen urges us to take a universal view on justice. He argues that when we avoid being parochial and strive to be impartial we will find that there will be much agreement that certain things are unjust. To reach this impartial perspective, Sen suggests we borrow Adam Smith's notion of the impartial spectator. Imagining the view of the impartial spectator we can see that some things are wrong, even if we do have a perfectly formed system of justice.[9] The impartial spectator is also a way of circumventing our tendency to enshrine local prejudices.

As I noted in the introduction, it is hard to say who is impartial. This was recently seen in discussions about the 2003 Iraq War. Perhaps discussion is one key element in deciding about justice. To repeat, Sen argues that we can have a strong sense that something is unjust without being able to agree on the exact reason or reasons why it is unjust. We can see that it is unjust even if we do not have a precise definition of justice. He uses the Iraq war as an example. Sen gives four different reasons for judging the Iraq war unjust. He suggests that it is unjust to invade a sovereign country without the approval of the United Nations. Second, it was unjust to invade Iraq without being well-informed about the facts concerning weapons of mass destruction. Third, it was unjust to go to war given the amount of disinformation suggesting that Saddam Hussein was behind the attacks on the World Trade Center. Fourth, it was wrong to go to war given the consequences and in particular given the amount of instability and suffering that the war brought to Iraq and the region.[10]

As sympathetic as I am to Sen's claims about the Iraq War, I realize that there are some who disagree (mostly in the United States), even now, and see the war as just. Rather than hope for an impartial spectator, perhaps we should seek a more informed spectator. In the introduction I argued that Michael Sandel's discussion of justice is parochial, but I do have some sympathy for his belief that our views on justice come out of the time and place where we live. Today, however, as Sandel's popularity in China illustrates, not to mention the demonstrations demanding democracy in the Middle East, ideas, particularly discussions of justice, have a global reach. Our lives are connected to the lives of others all over the world and sometimes we are disconnected from those who live in close proximity to us. We can and should broaden our understanding of justice by conversing with and learning from others and the lives they lead.

Sen is, I believe, right to insist that we can recognize injustice without having a perfectly formulated notion of what justice might be. Even more important for my purposes is Sen's claim that we must listen to a variety of views before making up our mind. Public discussion is a key factor in determining what is just. Certainly we can never decide if a social arrangement is just without listening to all who are affected by that arrangement. Part of what this book aims to do is to listen to and report on what the poor are saying. Instead of seeking an impartial spectator, I suggest seeking a *less parochial spectator*. We will never reach impartiality, but we can constantly work at being better informed by talking with those whose views and life circumstances differ from our own. This will not lead us to an impartial judgment, but it will mitigate against making a judgment based on false or incomplete information.

MORALITY, THE "GREAT MISTRESS OF SEDUCTION"

Ethical theory can be useful in helping us respond to the savage inequalities of our day, but let me cite yet another challenge that has been brought against ethical deliberation. Calling morality "the greatest mistress of seduction" and comparing it to the Greek muse Circe, who turns all of Odysseus' men to swine, Nietzsche argues that morality has many means of frightening off critical inquires, but its most potent weapon is its ability to seduce. With the help of Hermes, Odysseus withstands Circe's spells and forces Circe to reverse her spell on his men. No longer swine, Circe's charms still hold a certain sway over Odysseus and his crew. They while away another year with her, feasting on her food, drinking her wine and probably enjoying other pleasures before setting off again.[11] Nietzsche is a strange thinker to invoke a treatise that aims to think about ethical responsibility and inequality. He himself spoke out, at times, in favor of slavery and oppression. I doubt he would have had much sympathy for this project, but everyone who attempts to think about ethics should grapple with Nietzsche's critiques of ethical thinking. He insightfully warns of many of the pitfalls into which ethical thought can fall.

Nietzsche notes that almost everyone, even anarchists, makes their arguments through references to morality and orators never fail to use morality in their efforts to sway audiences. He labels the eighteenth century a time of moral fanaticism, and calls Rousseau the moral tarantula who bit both Kant and Robespierre. Even as Robespierre was presiding over the Reign of Terror, he was a moralist! In the middle of the regime of terror in 1794, he saw himself as bringing "an empire of wisdom, justice and virtue to earth."[12] As we marvel at Robespierre's delusion, we should consider our own. Today, we can add that Walmart and the United States on the eve of the Iraq invasion, to name just two recent examples, used morality to make their case. Recently Walmart's CEO announced on its website that through Walmart's transformation to the world's largest retailer "our culture of ethics and integrity has been a constant." He goes on: from the beginning, Walmart's culture of ethics and integrity "has defined who we are as a company, and how we as associates treat each other, our suppliers and our customers."[13] As we will document in chapter 3, there is plenty of evidence that contradicts these claims. Many claim that the company pays the majority of its workforce non-living wages, provides health insurance to less than half of its employees and is legendary for abandoning stores and leaving them to blight the landscape.

Listen to the appeals to morality and justice embedded in George W. Bush's speech announcing the invasion of Iraq in 2003:

First, Bush announces that this is a war to disarm a nation, "free" the people of Iraq, and defend the world from a grave danger.

> My fellow citizens. At this hour, American and coalition forces are in the early stages of military operations to disarm Iraq, to free its people and to defend the world from grave danger.[14]
> We will use war to bring peace and stop oppression:
> To all the men and women of the United States armed forces now in the Middle East, the peace of a troubled world and the hopes of an oppressed people now depend on you. That trust is well placed.[15]

The United States is leading a coalition that will preemptively attack a sovereign nation that is not threatening the United States, but Bush proclaims that it is Iraq that has no regard for the conventions of war. "In this conflict America faces an enemy that has no regard for conventions of war or rules of morality."[16] Bush also asserts that the war is justified because of the existence of weapons of mass destruction which Iraq did not have. He is announcing an attack on a regime that is not threatening the nation he leads, but

Iraq is the outlaw. He says he attacks "reluctantly," but he orders the United
Nations weapons inspectors to leave Iraq so that the war can begin.

> Our nation enters this conflict reluctantly, yet our purpose is sure. The people
> of the United States and our friends and allies will not live at the mercy of an
> outlaw regime that threatens the peace with weapons of mass murder. [17]

And finally, just in case one didn't get the point the first time, this is a war
but it is also the work of peace:

> My fellow citizens, the dangers to our country and the world will be overcome.
> We will pass through this time of peril and carry on the work of peace. We will
> defend our freedom. We will bring freedom to others and we will prevail. [18]

I have already admitted that ethics is an imprecise endeavor and that it is hard
to know with certainty what justice is. Almost everyone claims to be ethical
and almost all regimes claim to be just. All human beings are subject to
delusion. I suspect that Bush really thought the invasion of Iraq was a moral
and a just act. Moral appeals often deceive even those who make them in
good faith.

Even if we are not as deluded as Bush, all of us suffer from blind spots.
Talking with one another and listening to those who have different perspectives can lead us to rethink unjustified conclusions. There are a host of
philosophers today who are thinking about global inequalities and ethical
responsibility. In what follows I want to examine two of these thinkers whose
ideas I respect a great deal, Thomas Pogge and Peter Singer. All three of us
believe that global poverty is the most pressing moral issue of our day, but
our reasons for thinking this and therefore our thinking about our obligations
to address these savage inequalities differ.

Most of us agree that everyone should have the opportunity to succeed
and not be condemned to a life of poverty because of the accident of their
birth. Certainly we think that we should not be contributing to the poverty of
those born into it. Most believe we should not be wasting resources that the
next generation will need. As we drive our cars, we may believe that we
should not emit greenhouse gases if they contribute to environmental problems for poor third world farmers and our grandchildren. These principles are
relatively unproblematic, but many of us, indeed most of us, are not living
according to our own ethical ideals. How then can theory help us not only see
our duty, but actually do it?

POSITIVE RIGHTS—TOO FINE A DISTINCTION?

Today, many argue that the study of justice is fundamentally divided from the study of ethics, or individual comportment. For Thomas Pogge it is a *fait accompli*. "Justice" is the moral assessment of social rules such as laws, practices, social conventions, and institutions. Justice is only rarely used to assess the morality of an individual's or a group's conduct or character.[19] To say this another way, Pogge has an institutional and not an interactional understanding of justice. This means that human rights, for example, are primarily guaranteed by institutional arrangements and not by individual acts.

For Aristotle as for most great ethical thinkers, while it is important for the individual to be ethical, it is "finer and more divine" for cities and peoples to become ethical. His treatise strives to give an account of ethical comportment that will lead to a flourishing society. Both Aristotle and Plato stressed the interconnection between the ethical and the just society. In fact, for both of them, ethical-political theory was the most important philosophical occupation. Plato's literary creation, Diotima, says in the *Symposium* that the correct ordering of cities is the highest and most beautiful product of thought and then gives a vision of how one transforms her or his erotic drives into a force that brings justice to the state.[20] They are far from the only ones to have recognized the importance of tying ethics to the just ordering of social life. Lao-Tzu warned of the dangers of materialism and luxury goods even before Plato did, because Lao-Tzu worried about the social strife that such luxuries would bring. Confucius repeatedly stresses that justice can be brought about through the actions of an individual. The individual acts in such a way that motivates others to act in ethical ways. In short, in many traditions the ethical and the just are intimately tied. The ultimate goal of an ethical life is the creation of a just society.

For Pogge our responsibility is to insure that institutions are just. This division between individual comportment and just institutional ordering makes a certain amount of sense, but does it let middle-class people off too easily? Middle-class people the world over are deeply implicated in the systems that create and maintain poverty, because we benefit from them. Our discussions of justice should involve not only laws, social conventions and institutions, but also how we as individuals support and profit from unjust social arrangements and what we owe because of the benefits we receive.[21]

Pogge argues, and I agree, that it is the preeminent moral task of our time to ensure that all human beings have access to "minimally adequate shares of basic freedoms and . . . of drink, clothing, shelter, education and healthcare."[22] But Pogge is concerned that there is little support for the notion that those of us who are wealthy owe something to any particular poor person. He tries to get around the objections of those who claim that they are under no obligation to help the poor obtain food, clothing, shelter, education and health care by arguing that human rights should be seen "primarily as claims on coercive social institutions and secondarily as claims against those who uphold such institutions."[23] In other words, Pogge is arguing that social institutions are the main culprits in the denying of human rights and that individuals are responsible for the denying of human rights only to the extent that they uphold these institutions. Pogge offers us an elegant response to those who claim that the wealthy have no obligation to the poor. He suggests insofar as we support unfair social institutions we are denying others' rights. He urges us to work to change unjust social institutions and in addition to calculate how much we have benefitted from unjust social arrangements and then to make amends by giving to charity.

Contemporary philosophers have spilled a great deal of ink arguing over the distinction between positive and negative rights.[24] A positive right is the right to something—for example, to education, health care or a job. A negative right is the right not to be interfered with—for example, the right to choose my religion (or to choose no religion at all), to speak my mind or to not have my property taken away from me arbitrarily. The right is negative in the sense that it does not entitle me to anything. It only insures that no one unjustly interferes in my private affairs. Some philosophers have argued that our duties to others are limited to noninterference, but we are not obligated to help others reach even a minimal standard of living. Critics of positive rights argue that it might be very nice for the rich to aid the poor, but the poor do not have the right to demand that aid. Pogge himself does not hold this view, but he believes that it is not only philosophers who believe that the poor have no right to demand help.[25] Pogge argues that this is a widely shared view, even among the general public, so he carefully constructs his arguments so as to avoid reference to positive rights. He argues that we have a responsibility to change the unfair institutions that are responsible for much of the poverty in the world today.

As Jiwei Ci points out, Pogge's institutional approach requires us to develop a bad conscience for acts that we did not do as individuals.[26]Ci suggests that it is not an easy thing to develop a bad conscience when we have not personally committed the wrong, but have merely benefited from unjust institutional arrangements. He argues that there are few societies where a sense of responsibility for institutions is a part of one's moral education. When we reflect upon our moral responsibility we inevitably think about what we as individuals have done. It will not be easy to get individuals to accept blame for the harm institutions have done especially when one has not personally endorsed the institution. On the one hand, those of us who live in democracies have the right to express our views and lobby for change, but on the other hand, any individual's power often seems miniscule compared, for example, to the power of the agricultural lobby, both in the United States and in Europe. One of the greatest challenges to achieving social justice in to-day's world is the impotence that individuals feel when faced with unjust institutions.

I admire Pogge's work. He is certainly right to stress that world poverty has a great deal to do with unjust institutions and that we should work to change these institutions. This distinction between social institutions and individuals is a useful one, as is the distinction between negative and positive rights, but this ideal distinction does not precisely fit what is happening in the real world. We will see that people the world over have been wronged so that I might fill my car's gas tank and people the world over will suffer from the greenhouse gases my automobile produces. As Pogge himself realizes, there is so much exploitation involved in the extraction of minerals that a strong case can be made that my tank is filled in large part thanks to traffic in stolen property.

To repeat Nietzsche's warning, morality has great seductive power. If we are not careful, the seemingly clear distinction between positive and negative rights can actually obscure how wealth—even the wealth of the middle class—is often the product of exploitation and thus it is not unambiguously mine. To the extent that what I own is tainted and not unambiguously mine, most would say that I do not have any positive rights at all. The reality of our moral world is more complex than the overly precise dichotomy between negative and positive rights suggests. I am struck by how many times in my day systemic imbalances aid me at the expense of the poor. In this age of globalization, our lives are purchased not only at the cost of great suffering to those living next to mineral wealth, but also by workers far away as well as the nearly invisible workers very close to home, such as the ones cooking food and washing dishes in restaurants or cleaning offices. If I fuel my car with oil that has been extracted at great cost to the people of the Niger Delta I have harmed them, or at least benefited from the harm imposed upon them. Even if the oil in my tank is not from the Niger Delta, world oil supplies are often tight and the oil that is being pumped in the Delta, and many other places around the world at great cost to the local population, is helping to keep the price of the oil in my tank low. If I shop at a store that does not pay some of its employees a living wage am I not being unethical by benefiting from an institution that is unjust? Am I really entitled to the shirt or the milk if exploitation makes my acquisition of the product possible?[27]

The examples Pogge uses to explain his point are telling. He argues that it would be unjust to support a society that enslaved blacks, disenfranchised women, or mistreated servants.[28] Pogge writes about countries where ser-vants suffer from lack of legal protections or where legal protections are in place but ineffective:

> Servants are also often forced to endure illegal conduct on account of econom-
> ic necessity: they do not dare file complaints against their employers for fear
> of being fired. This fear is both justified and substantial. They often have only
> minimal financial resources and no other place to spend the night, there may
> be a general oversupply of servants, and they may have reason to believe that
> their present employer would refuse to issue them the favorable reference they
> need to find new employment.[29]

I imagine that many might read this passage and think of a country in the Persian Gulf or South Asia, but it also applies to the United States today, in particular to undocumented workers. How easy it is to recognize oppression perpetuated by those living far away and at the same time to overlook the ways in which the current structure of society privileges us. I grant that there are workers who are laboring in virtual slavery in some places in the Middle East as well as other parts of the world. As we will see in chapter 3, particularly among the undocumented workers in the United States, there are those whose working conditions do not differ that much from the conditions Pogge describes. There is, naturally, a difference between hiring someone and exploiting them personally and buying orange juice from a bottler who has bought oranges from a grower who in turn hired exploited undocumented workers, but still my ownership is not unproblematic.

Documented workers in the United States are usually not treated as badly as undocumented workers, but to the extent the Walmart workers, fast food workers or any number of other service industry workers in the United States do not make a living wage or do not have health care, one could argue that laws of the United States are enabling me to take unfair advantage of these people.

Pogge writes that to have a human right means that "insofar as reasonably possible" social institutions are designed so that individuals have access to them.[30] What is reasonable? The exploited worker in the orange groves of Florida might have something to teach me about how far I should go to redress his or her exploitation. Pogge is correct, in my view, that institutions must change so that the global poor have more opportunities. He also suggests that as individuals we need to figure out how much we have benefited from these unjust institutions and make amends. There is so much that is unjust about the institutions that support even middle-class lives that I fear all overly sharp distinctions can obscure the complexity of our lives. Rather than draw hard distinctions about how to understand our moral responsibilities, we should keep questioning our place in the world, the underpinnings of our lives and what this implies about our ethical responsibilities.

Nietzsche teaches us that genealogy is essential to understand morality.[31] In other words, to judge the worth of moral theory we must examine how it has evolved. To construct his genealogy of morals, Nietzsche looks to prehistory. He imagines that in some undefined, perhaps prehistoric time, the strong called themselves "good" and labeled the weak "bad." Judaism and Christianity represent for him the rise of underhanded moralities. Under the auspices of these moral systems, weaker men subverted the power of the strong. The weak labeled themselves "good" and called the strong "evil" and produced bad conscience in the strong. Bad conscience was invented by priests to weaken the strong (but paradoxically it made the strong more interesting). These priests taught asceticism, that is, the renouncing of world-ly pleasures in return for otherworldly rewards. They revalued the system that favored the strong, bound up the strong in the chains of morality and reinvented the moral code to their own advantage. The teaching of pity (*Mitleid*) also masked an attempt by the weak to conquer the strong. In short, theories of morality and justice are merely ruses in the game of trying to dominate others. The priests, weak by nature but wily, taught the people to be submissive and subverted the strong, and they did it under the guise of ethical concern.

Nietzsche thought a great deal about the utilitarian claim that morality consists in maximizing happiness. He argues that as long as the utility that reigns in moral values is the utility of the herd, there can be no true love of neighbor.[32] Care for the herd leads to the neglect of the great individual. Humans flourish when we challenge one another, not when we allow the "weak" to survive. The command to love one's neighbor masks fear of neighbor. As soon as society secures itself against external dangers, it sees many of the strong and dangerous drives that it once prized in its citizens as dangerous. Society when it is at war encourages qualities such as daring, revenge, slyness, rapacity and the desire to rule its members, but these things are discouraged as soon as societies are at peace. The more secure a society has become against outside intruders, the more it prizes sheep and lambs, i.e., citizens who have given themselves to the herd. The herd sees independent spirits as dangerous and labels everything that stands out from the herd as "evil."

Theories of morality seduce because they often convince us of the right-eousness of our own acts and the evil of our opponents. As I have already said, I do not doubt that Bush really believed the Iraq war was justified as Robespierre was convinced of the morality of his acts. Pogge disparages those who cynically use moral justifications as a mere cover for their acts, as do I, but I also worry about the possibility that morality can seduce all of those who make recourse to it.[33]

There is precious little evidence that contradicts Nietzsche's prediction of the coming of herd mentality. Our failure to aid others may have a great deal to do with a capitalist marketplace constantly telling us that happiness can be found in consumption and drives us, like cattle, to buy our way to bliss. Even the relatively wealthy have gotten used to ignoring the suffering of the world. We are convinced that happiness lies in the owning of a Lexus (especially those of us who cannot afford one), the pleasure of an expensive meal or the buying of new clothes even if the clothes we have are far from worn out. We indulge in these pleasures—that is, whatever pleasures our maxed out credit cards will allow—usually without giving much thought to the people who sew our clothes or wash our cars. Given the intensely capitalist marketplace in which we in the United States live (as well as many in the Third World), it is not surprising that we have come to believe that happiness is found in consuming. Nietzsche believed that devotion to otherworldly rewards represents a sickness and that superior people embrace this life as opposed to living for rewards in the next, but he also recognizes that the herd comportment that typifies bourgeois life hardly constitutes an embrace of life.

We have also become convinced that our wealth is deserved and that poverty is a personal failure. Nietzsche shows us how often morality can be used as a way for some to let themselves off the hook and blame the victim. The logic of the ascetic priests can be found in many of the arguments that are currently used to implore the wealthy to give more to charity. Looking at the problem of poverty in terms of charity obscures how even the middle class benefits from the current structuring of globalization as well as the ways in which inequality within the United States is a product of systemic inequalities. To cite but one example, financing schools in the United States through local taxes is bound to ensure that poor communities will have inferior schools. An individual tutoring a poor child in the United States does not make up for a system which insures that poor children will attend inferior schools. On an international scale, trade agreements that secure the free flow of capital offer benefits to international banks and first world pension funds, but they often harm citizens of third world countries. Sending a few dollars to a charity in Indonesia does nothing to make up for the masses that were thrown into poverty during the East Asian crisis of the 1990s. I will go into these problems in more detail in chapter 3, but even the International Monetary Fund now admits that the crisis was exacerbated by the policies it imposed on these East Asian countries. These policies helped to ensure that Western bank loans were repaid, but literally caused millions to fall into poverty.

One of the most troubling aspects about the treatment of African Americans under slavery was their ruthless exploitation. With little regard for their health and well-being, African Americans were first enslaved and then subjected to obvious discrimination after slavery. Even today African Americans in the United States suffer from much greater poverty than whites, and they trail whites in almost every measure of public health. Nietzsche writes that, although it offends many to hear it, a healthy aristocracy accepts not only slavery, but the sacrifice of masses of people as well. [34] I doubt many slave masters shared Nietzsche's views, at least not openly. Slaveholders often argued that African Americans were not fully human.

Some of the pro-slavery rhetoric was couched in terms of protecting African Americans who were not capable of looking out for themselves. Another justification that most of us no longer maintain, at least consciously—as Nietzsche did—was that blacks are more capable of bearing pain than white people are.[35] Few, if any say, as Nietzsche does, that we would accept the sacrifice of a mass of people, but many are living in great affluence while many others live in great poverty. In practice, however, we do accept the sacrifice of many to support our lifestyles.

Philosophical discourses can be used to disguise systems of privilege. Theory can be used to obscure one's responsibilities and obscure the obvious. Abstract reflection can turn us into Hamlets so lost in contemplation that we fail to act. Ethical theory can become an end in itself; that is, it can become a complex mental game that occupies our time, but never influences how we live our lives. Ethical theory can be and has been used to justify the most outrageous actions. Precisely because ethical visions can take us out of the realm of the conventional they can be dangerous. For every Buddha, there is a Robespierre. At their best, ethical visions challenge us and awake us from our dogmatic slumber, but departing from the norm always entails risks. Many revolutions have gone wrong, but ethical and social justice theory, prudently applied, can illuminate the errors of our traditional ways and bring about positive social change. Philosophers are famous for their exaggerated use of reason and overanalyzing or analyzing in place of acting, but moral philosophy can free us from the commonly accepted, but unreflected wisdom of the day. Where would the world be without visionaries who question conventional wisdom? Almost every evil that one can imagine has been widely accepted, sometimes for thousands of years. To the extent that theory can shake the perceived wisdom, unsettle our herdlike demeanor, and cause us to act to reduce the vast and unnecessary human suffering of this world it is risky, but we are wise to try it even while we remain vigilant to its seductive wiles.

Peter Singer, who is a major inspiration for this work, argues that reason has an important role to play in the development of ethical views and that ethical thinking necessarily takes a universal point of view. He alleges that this is true for a wide variety of ethical thinkers, from Plato to Sartre.

> Ethics requires us to go beyond "I" and "you" to the universal law, the universalizable judgment, the standpoint of the impartial spectator or ideal observer, or whatever we choose to call it.[36]

For Singer, to think ethically means to realize, at the very least, that my own interests cannot count for more simply because they are my interests. Ethics requires us to ask not merely what is good for me, but what is good for others as well. He argues that ethical thinking requires us to think of others and therefore utilitarianism is the first step in all moral thinking. It is the first step because it asks the very basic question of what kind of effect an act will have on the interests of everyone involved. Other ethical theories may go further and argue, for example, that individual rights, certain notions of justice, the sanctity of life, or a standard of purity is the key to ethics. To the extent that such systems are universal they are ethical, but they go beyond utilitarianism. Singer believes that utilitarianism asks the most basic question of how our actions affect others. In addition to asking how my actions will affect the actions of others, other ethical theories posit some higher good that all must achieve. For example, Singer does not believe that the sanctity of life is an absolute value. If someone is suffering and wishes to end their own life the key question for Singer would be "How does this decision affect others?" Utilitarianism demands that we consider the happiness of everyone, not just the happiness of ourselves.

Singer is not arguing that we must treat everyone impartially. He writes that there are good reasons for showing partiality towards one's family. The parent-child bond is so strong that the attempts by the Israeli kibbutz to raise children communally had to be abandoned. Allowing parents to show partiality towards their own children seems to be the best way to ensure that children receive the care they need. This is particularly true today when states seem to be doing less and less for their citizens.[37] Some partiality is then justified on the grounds that everyone benefits from it in the end.

Even Singer admits that reason alone cannot ground morality. With Hume, he acknowledges that in ethics we begin with what we want and then use reason as a means to achieving our wants. Reason can give us the best means to achieve an end, but reason alone cannot give us a reason to be moral. Reason alone cannot justify valuing the well-being of others. But can reason even give us the best means to achieve our ends? For example, we may agree with Singer's claim that absolute poverty is a bad thing, but be unsure about what we should do about that fact. Should we give to CARE or Oxfam? How much should we give? Should we give to a local food bank or should we give to a person begging on the streets? Should we see, as I have already suggested, that the whole discourse of charity risks obscuring the ways we are implicated in the production of poverty? It may be more important, as Pogge suggests, to work for institutional changes. But again, once we decide that institutions must change, reason can lead reasonable people in different directions. Reason tells us, as I have already mentioned, that the IMF made serious mistakes in its handling of the East Asian crisis, but it is more difficult to know how we should act to change the current structure—both within our nation and within the world—in order to insure that the poor truly have the opportunity to rise out of poverty.

The step from theory to actions is tricky. As we will see in more detail in the next chapter, Singer himself attests to this difficulty by repeatedly shifting his prescriptions about how much we should be giving to reduce poverty. In some places, he calls upon people to give 1 percent of their earnings to fight global poverty. In another place, he calls upon people to give 10 percent of their earnings. In his most recent work, he argues for a sliding scale and asks very little of those who make less than $100,000.[38]

Singer argues that it is in our self-interest to care about others and that it in no way diminishes ethical acts, that caring for others is part of what makes life worth living. Kant argues that an act has no true moral value unless it is done purely out of duty. Singer suggests that acting ethically can be pleasurable and this is an important part of the reason why we choose to do it. He also argues that the study of ethics has long been tied to religion. It is only since the twentieth century that ethics has been studied by itself. Citing Derek Parfit, Singer holds out the hope that divorcing religion from ethics will lead to great progress in ethics. In particular, he believes that divorcing ethics from religious faith will lead to a broad consensus about what is ethical.[39] I doubt religion itself is the problem. Most of the great religions of the world have spent a considerable amount of effort thinking about how we should treat one another and their thoughts on these matters often mirror Singer's conclusions. At times Singer himself realizes that many religions offer support to his views and he himself even cites religious figures to suggest the universality of the ethical impulse to treat others with charity.[40]

After Nietzsche, it is hard not to look with suspicion at the motives behind the moralist and for the ways in which our rational acts are secretly guided by the passions. Schopenhauer, from whom Nietzsche learned a great deal, has a particularly insightful critique of reason.[41] Reason, for Schopenhauer, is the author of any abstract thought. So religious dogmas, to the extent that they are abstractions, represent the work of reason as do the theories of philosophers. Abstraction is possible, Schopenhauer argues, only to the extent that we possess language. Language allows us to remove ourselves from the present and to consider the world in the abstract. This ability to abstract is for Schopenhauer one of our greatest abilities. It is the basis for language, and language allows us to plan and to coordinate our actions with others. Humans are capable of showing courage in the face of injury or even death precisely because we can use reason to distance ourselves from the present dangers. At the same time, reason makes mistakes—for example, the claim that the earth is the center of the universe—that last for thousands of years.

For Schopenhauer, there is something dreamlike in reason. Indeed, all those engaged in ethical reflections should be haunted by the possibility that they may be producing abstractions gone terribly wrong, or at least abstractions that miss the mark. Even the most cursory glance at the history of philosophy shows that very intelligent people have used rational arguments to advance theories that we would consider today to be implausible and even outrageous. I have already mentioned Aristotle's defense of slavery and his pervasive misogyny as examples, in my view, of reason gone wrong. There was reason, however misguided, in the IMF proscriptions for East Asia during the East Asian crisis of the 1990s. Even as I call upon reason to help make my case, I look for ways to curb reason's excesses. To recognize reason's limits in no way implies the necessity to reject reason altogether. Audre Lorde argues, in a very beautiful essay, that feeling is the deepest source of knowledge.[42] It is, no doubt, an important source, but it also has its limits. Feelings often alert us to deficiencies in reason. Much of the power of Singer's analysis comes from his dissection of how frivolous our spending habits are when compared to the plight of the world's poor, but it is probably naïve to think that a transfer of wealth would solve the problem and that the world's wealthy might be convinced to do it. Pogge is probably right that this global poverty is largely a systemic problem and that the solution will only come with changes that take power from wealthy elites and put it in the hands of the poor.

Andrew Kuper has debated Singer over the question of whether or not giving to charity is the best way to fulfill our moral obligation to the poor. Kuper argues that a theory which does not include a "contextual and institutional analysis risks offering nothing more than a cosmetic fix." It may even make things worse if it props up a corrupt regime. More than charity, Kuper argues, we need good governance and better markets.[43] Kuper is right that aid can sometimes make things worse, but as we will see in chapter 2, there is a great awareness of this and there are many efforts to ensure that aid is used more effectively. The fact that reason sometimes or even often fails to predict the outcome of charitable efforts is no reason to conclude that reason can never guide charity to a successful outcome. And there are certainly many cases where political change has not worked out well! Even if Kuper is right about good governance being more important than charity, there is no reason why we shouldn't give something to effective charities while we work to change systems that encourage and support bad governance. I favor the use of argumentation, but question the ability of reason to articulate our duty or the just *definitively*. Reason makes its attempt. We learn from that attempt. We revise our behavior and advocate for changes in social arrangements and think some more. Reason is too crude an instrument to deliver final moral edicts when it comes to the ever-changing ways of the world. There are good reasons to do as Singer suggests and give money to help alleviate poverty. I also endorse Pogge's call to work for systemic change.

As I have already said, Sen, who is both an economist and a philosopher, (and as Singer notes in response to Kuper, the head of Oxfam) suggests that we eschew comprehensive theories of justice in favor of Adam Smith's impartial spectator.[44] Sen argues that we do not need a comprehensive or ideal theory to see that some things are wrong. This impartial spectator can see for a number of reasons that something is unjust without knowing exactly what perfect justice might be. We can see, for example, for a number of reasons that we should act to end severe poverty. We do not need to have a fully formed theory of justice to come to that conclusion. We do not need a fully formed theoretical model of justice to know that there is something seriously wrong in the way that resources are distributed in this world. The more we learn about how wealthy nations have set the rules of international trade to benefit themselves at great cost to poorer nations—and that even the middle class reaps benefits from this—the clearer our duty to act to redress these wrongs will become.

But knowing that something is wrong does not ensure that we know exactly what should be done to correct the situation. Sen suggests impartial reason can show us that something is unjust, but is incapable of giving us a fully formed theory of justice. Sen also stresses that we must be prepared to accept that there can be competing reasonable understandings of what would be the just thing to do. Reason cannot tell us exactly what we need to do in response to the savage inequalities of our time. Some measures such as reducing our carbon footprint and giving to charity might be obvious. That said, the more we look at how much of the current world order disadvantages the poor, and most importantly the more we listen to the poor themselves, the more clarity we may be able to gain about how to go about redressing the problems, but reasonable people can and do disagree.

COBBLING TOGETHER AN ETHICS: CONCENTRATING ON OUTCOMES AND USING REASON, EMOTION, AND DIALOGUE

The world has seen some remarkable success in the reduction of poverty, for example, in South Korea, parts of China, Kerala, and many places in Indonesia. Taking a longer view, the Nordic countries of Europe were very poor until relatively recently. Smallpox has been eliminated, great strides have been made against polio and river blindness, and the world is slowly turning to address malaria, AIDS, and tuberculosis. Theory can give us a vision of the just and motivation to do the right thing, but choosing the ethical and just course requires in-depth study of the particularities of the situation at hand. Once we decide on a course of action we must closely examine whether the measures introduced to mitigate the injustice are having their intended effects. As Sen argues, fairness must be judged not only on the basis of abstract principles, but more importantly on the basis of the outcomes the principles produce. [45]

We will have to cobble together a guide for living and a plan for change in this world of savage inequalities from a number of different sources.

Reason will be a resource, but so will our sentiments. It is dangerous to trust our moral instincts too much. Some slave owners may have genuinely felt that the subjugation of blacks was justified and probably they felt deeply that the races should remain separate. Many people today feel deeply that homosexuality is wrong, but others feel just as deeply that it is not. People feel deeply about abortion, but have very different views about the ethics of that practice. Whose feelings correspond to the moral? It is particularly important to question our sentiments when our reasons suggest that we need to make some possibly painful sacrifices.

How do we question our feelings? One way to question our feelings is to ask how others feel. Dialogue with others may give us new vistas for understanding the limits of our perspectives. We cannot rely on our feelings alone to guide us in moral decisions, but even if it were possible to remove our feelings from our deliberations about morals it would not be a good idea. Our feelings should play a role in the grounding and development of our ethics as should reason. Feelings are one source of knowledge and we should not dismiss them any more than we should uncritically accept them.

Social conditioning should not be seen as merely clouding or masking true ethics. We should scrutinize received wisdom, but not ignore it. Furthermore, we should collect perceived wisdom from many sources. Philosophers need to read social scientists and economists as well as visit slums and talk with the poor. Philosophers bring our experience in thinking about ethics and justice to the table, and then in our discussions with others we try to see how these ideas can be realized or we may see how they need to be modified. Our moral thinking is inevitably shaped by the times and places in which we live, and the people we have known, and so ethics has evolved and will continue to evolve. The fight against world poverty, the civil rights movement, various antiwar movements, the women's rights movement, the ecological movement, the struggle for gay rights and the anticolonial movement are moral issues that have deeply resonated with me. Others would compose different lists, seeing other issues as important and discounting some of the issues I see as relevant. There is nothing wrong with that. Disagreement and dialogue are good signs when it comes to ethics. These movements were broad coalitions where those who were not directly affected by the wrong joined the movement to help correct the wrong.

Traditionally, it is claimed that the story of Western philosophy begins with Thales, who was renowned not only for his understandings of the heavens, but also for falling into a well because he was gazing at the stars and not watching his step. Philosophers have often taken it as a point of pride that they do not think about the world before their eyes, but see another more profound reality, far removed from the everyday. Plato's Socrates discusses Thales' fall in the *Theaetetus*. There, Socrates defends Thales from the ridicule of a Thracian servant girl who says that the great philosopher knew the things of the heavens, but not the things in front of him or at his feet.[46] Philosophers don't know how to make a bed, flavor a dish or make a flattering speech. They don't ask whether this person is happy or whether this action is just, but instead the philosopher asks, "What are happiness and justice in general?" This vision of philosophy is telling in many ways. Plato's Socrates claims that the servant girl had very little understanding of Thales because Thales was devoted to understanding what a human being is and how one should act and be acted upon. In other words, it is important to study and understand people and not just the movements of the heavens, and Socrates claims that Thales was an expert in understanding people. Aristotle also argues that Thales understood this world very well and was not simply lost in the stars. He writes that Thales, after his fall, used his knowledge of the heavens to predict the weather and made a fortune speculating by renting out all of the olive presses in a year when he saw that there would be a bumper crop. Thales was not really interested in the money, but rather, tired of the ridicule heaped on philosophers, he wanted to show that he understood the things of this world. Aristotle was vehement in his moral condemnation of monopolies, but as long as the point was to show the philosopher's acumen in the things of this world he was willing to cast his moral scruples aside.[47] Aristotle clearly revels in the story of Thales' revenge.

How might the servant girl have replied to Socrates? Might she have said that the one who makes the philosopher's bed and cleans the philosopher's house knows a great deal about people? Might she have said that the servant knows at least some of the realities of this earth that the philosopher often misses? Unfortunately, the servant's girl remark is reported by the philosopher, but she never gets a chance to air her views fully in Plato's dialogue.

We have learned to live with, and in some sense accept, enormous inequalities as somehow justified. It is difficult to reconstruct a fourth-century BC servant's point of view, but what about those who live on the margins of today's society? What about the janitor who cleans our office, the dishwasher in the restaurant where we have eaten, or the worker in China who sews our clothes? What about the worker in East Asia who has lost his or her job and food subsidies because of IMF policies or the fisherman from the Niger Delta who can no longer fish because the extraction of oil has ruined the fishing grounds? These people can speak, and if they happen to speak another language, there are many who will translate their words into our language. One way to check the extravagances of theory and the lethargy of social custom is to listen to voices that have often been excluded from theoretical discourses. If one seeks to help others, it is particularly important to listen to the people one is trying to help.

One of the reasons that we do not do more about the poverty in the world is that it is often obscured. Most of us in the United States live in close proximity to poverty, but often do not see it. There is a concerted effort today by some journalists and other writers to make it more visible. Most of us would agree that poverty is a bad thing and that those of us who are in a position to ameliorate human suffering caused by poverty should do so, but we are not doing all that we should because we are not constantly confronted with it and we do not know exactly what to do about it. Dialogue is not only a way to check theory; it is also a way to bring us into contact with those who we often overlook. Listening to the voices of those who are on the other side of the great wealth divide will be crucial to helping us understand and meet our obligations to others.

I almost wish I could deliver a simple ethics—some neat little package of dos and don'ts—that would assure you that you are being ethical in this age when some of us have so much, while others lack the basic necessities. I cannot. In what follows I will try to show how even middle-class people, the world over, are often benefiting from some of the same things that are active-ly harming the poor. I can begin to suggest some of the ways we might try to work to change the systems that produce and maintain this poverty. I hope to add to the conversation about what middle-class people owe to the poor by pointing out the myriad of ways that middle-class people benefit from the exploitation of the poor. I will also point out ways that some of what harms the poor of the world harms the middle class as well. Every middle-class person is in a different place and that place is constantly shifting over the course of our lives. Some have much more time and money than others. At different times in our lives we are in better positions to work on this problem. Everyone has to think about where they are and how much time and effort they have to help rid this world of the scourge of poverty. Moral crusades are almost never a good idea. I do not think that we should demand too much of ourselves, but it seems to me that most of us can take modest steps—give some of our time and some of our money in an effort to improve the lives of the poor. I even think our lives will be richer and more rewarding if we try. At the same time, we have friends and family and if we give too much time and financial resources to others we may risk neglecting those close at hand. As the great recession of 2008 dramatically proved, the middle class in the West is not secure and the middle class in the rest of the world is even less secure. Each person must think about their life and the multiple relationships that are important to them and then also think about the poor.

It has been suggested to me that my approach might be called "an ethics of awareness." This seems like a good label. It is, as I have already said cobbled together. It borrows from many thinkers and rejects the notion that any school of thought has the final word when it comes to identifying a correct formula for ethical action. Formulas do not take into account the constant change of our lives. Those of us who live relatively privileged lives should become aware of those who struggle and think about how we might go about helping those who live in poverty. We should awaken ourselves from the dogmatic slumber that has lulled us into assuming that distant poverty—or not too distant poverty—is too massive and too far removed for us to do anything about it. There are ways we can act that will not cost us a great deal and these actions will contribute to ending the worst global poverty.

Remembering Aristotle's claim that ethical theory is inherently imprecise and always tied to the contingencies of the moment as well as Nietzsche's claim that ethical arguments are often self-serving ruses, let us think about what we can do, not merely to interpret the world, but to make it a better place! Let us seek after wisdom by talking with those who have been excluded and constantly questioning the perceived wisdom, and then let us act!

NOTES

1. Karl Marx "Theses on Feurbach" https://www.marxists.org/archive/marx/works/1845/theses/theses.htm

2. There is a rich philosophical literature dealing with ethical and social issues surrounding inequality. John Rawls' *A Theory of Justice* is the most influential work on social ethics written in the last 100 years. See *A Theory of Justice* (Cambridge: Harvard University Press, 1971). A later restatement and in some important ways modification of Rawls' position can be found in his *The Law of Peoples* (Cambridge: Harvard University Press, 2001). In Rawls' wake a number of scholars have written about the ethical issues surrounding poverty and the unequal distribution of resources both within nations and between nations. In particular, I admire the work of Thomas Pogge, Amartya Sen and Peter Singer. See Thomas Pogge *World Development and Human Rights* (Cambridge, UK: Polity, 2002) and more recently *Politics as Usual* (Cambridge, UK: Polity 2009). Pogge has also edited a number of volumes devoted to global poverty; see *Global Justice* (Oxford, UK: Blackwell, 2001) and *Global Institutions and Responsibilities: Achieving Global Justice* (Malden MA: Blackwell, 2005). Sen has developed the Capabilities Approach showing us how poverty and well-being must be measured in terms of capabilities and not merely income. *Development as Freedom* (Oxford: Oxford University Press, 1999) is merely one of Sen's most famous works on this subject. Most recently he has published *The Idea of Justice* (Cambridge: Harvard University Press, 2009) and (with Jean Dreze) *An Uncertain Glory: India and its Contradictions* (Princeton NJ: Princeton University Press, 2013). For an extensive bibliography of Sen's important contributions see Polly Vizard's *Poverty and Human Rights: Sen's 'Capability Perspective' Explored* (Oxford: Oxford University Press, 2006). Singer has underlined Rawls' failure to think about poverty in a global context. He also stresses that individuals should take concrete steps to address global poverty. Three of Peter Singer's most important contributions to this area are "Famine, Affluence and Morality" *Philosophy and Public Affairs* 1, no. 3 (Spring 1972) and *One World* (New Haven: Yale University Press, 2002) and *The Life You Can Save* (New York: Random House, 2009). Other works include Onora O'Neill *Bounds of Justice* (Cambridge UK: Cambridge University Press, 2000). Kai Nielson *Globalization and Justice* (Amherst, New York: Humanity Books, 2003). Martha Nussbaum *Sex and Social Justice* (New York: Oxford University Press, 1999). Richard W. Miller *Globalizing Justice: The Ethics of Poverty and Power* (Oxford: Oxford University Press, 2010). This is a small sample of some important works in the field and I will be mentioning many others in the course of this book.

3. Aristotle, *The Politics and The Constitution of Athens* trans. Jowett, revised (New York: Cambridge University Press, 1996) book 1, chapter 5.

4. Ibid. book 1, chapter 13.

5. *Nicomachean Ethics* Book 1, chapter 4. I am using Terence Irwin's translation (Indianapolis: Hackett Publishing Company, 1999) Hereafter cited as NE.

6. NE Book 1, chapters 3 and 7. Book 2, chapter 2.

7. NE Book 2, chapter 2.

8. NE Book 6, chapter 5.

9. Amartya Sen *The Idea of Justice* (Cambridge MA: Harvard University Press, 2009).

10. *The Idea of Justice*, p. 3.

11. *Dawn: Thoughts on the Prejudices of Philosophy*, "Preface," 3.

12. Nietzsche mentions this in the preface to *Dawn* (section 3).

13. http://ethics.walmartstores.com/

14. Bush, George W. Untitled (Speech Announcing the beginning of Military Actions in Iraq) given on March 19, 2003. Found at "President Bush's Address on the Iraq Invasion," *Wall Street Journal* http://blogs.wsj.com/dispatch/2013/03/18/full-text-of-president-george-w-bushs-speech-march-19-2003/

15. Ibid.

16. Ibid.

17. Ibid.

18. Ibid.

19. *Politics as Usual: What Lies Behind the Pro-Poor Rhetoric*, pp. 14-16.

20. *Symposium* 209b

21. For a recent discussion of Pogge's views on these questions see Alison M. Jaggar ed. *Thomas Pogge and His Critics* (Cambridge: Polity, 2010).

22. *World Poverty and Human Rights*, p. 51.

23. *World Poverty and Human Rights*, p. 45.

24. Isaiah Berlin was one of the first to make the distinction between negative and positive liberty explicitly in his essay "Two Concepts of Liberty" in *Liberty: Incorporating Four Essays on Liberty* ed. Henry Hardy 2ed. (Oxford: Oxford, 2002) but the distinction has been made at least implicitly since Kant.

25. *Thomas Pogge and His Critics*, p. 195.

26. Jiwei Ci "What Negative Duties? Which Moral Universalism?" In *Thomas Pogge and His Critics*, p. 93.

27. Many have questioned the negative/positive rights distinction. See, for example, Henry Shue, *Basic Rights: Subsistence, Affluence, and U.S. Foreign Policy* 2nd ed. (Princeton: Princeton University Press, 1996). See also Charles Jones *Global Justice: Defending Cosmopolitanism* (Oxford UK: Oxford University Press, 1999) pp. 62-66. Jones' argument follows Shue in claiming that rights cannot be realized unless we all join in making sure we have these rights. He cites the example of free speech. One cannot possess that right unless others agree to help protect it. My argument is somewhat different. I argue, particularly when it comes to material possessions, our claims to ownership are often tainted. Given that we possess these tainted goods they are not unambiguously ours and we owe restitution to many who have been exploited so that we might have them. See also Elizabeth Ashford "The Alleged Dichotomy between Positive and Negative Rights and Duties" in Charles R. Beitz and Robert E. Goodin eds. *Global Basic Rights* (Oxford UK: Oxford University Press, 2009) pp. 92-112. Ashford argues for what she calls a substantive interdependence between the right to subsistence and other rights. Some, for example, have argued that it is never necessary to make recourse to positive rights. To those, for example, who worry that we must protect people from coercion, those who do not believe in positive rights suggest that coercion can be addressed simply by prohibiting it. Ashford points out that there may be times, for example, when one is very hungry, when it might make sense to allow one's self to be coerced so that they could gain food.

28. *World Poverty and Human Rights* p. 66.

29. *World Poverty and Human Rights* p. 63.

30. *World Poverty and Human Rights* p. 46.

31. Nietzsche writes about morality in most of his writings including *The Untimely, Meditations, Human All Too Human, Dawn, The Gay* Science, *Beyond Good and Evil*, and *Twilight of the Idols*. The brief synopsis I am giving here is drawn mainly from *Beyond Good and Evil*.

32. *Beyond Good and Evil* 201

33. *Politics as Usual* p. 150ff

34. *Beyond Good and Evil* 259

35. Nietzsche makes this claim in *On the Genealogy of Morals* (second essay, section 7).

36. *Practical Ethics,* p. 12.

37. Singer *How Are We to Live: Ethics in an Age of Self Interest* (Amherst, NY: Prometheus Books, 1995) pp. 95-97.

38. *The Life You Can Save* (Random House: New York, 2009)

39. Singer *How are We to Live* p. 15.

40. See, for example, *The Life You Can Save* pp 19-22.

41. *The World As Will and Representation* trans. E.F.J. Payne (Mineola: Dover, 1966)

42. Audre Lorde. "Uses of the Erotic: The Erotic as Power." *Sister Outsider: Essays and Speeches.* (Freedom, CA: Crossing Press, 1984) 53-59.

43. "Global Poverty Relief: More than Charity" in *Global Responsibilities: Who Must Deliver on Human Rights* ed. Andrew Kuper (New York: Routledge, 2005) p. 163. Another good discussion of the effectiveness of aid can be found in Cullity, *The Moral Demands of Affluence* (Oxford: Claredon Press Oxford, 2004) chapter 3.

44. *The Idea of Justice,* 44.

45. This is a point Sen has made repeatedly, most recently in *An Uncertain Glory: India and its Contradictions.* John Stuart Mill, an important utilitarian philosopher, makes a similar point when talking about the ethics of taxation. Mill asks what would be a fair form of taxation? One could, for example, tally up how much the services of the government would cost and then divide that number by the number of citizens. Wouldn't it be fair if everyone paid the same amount? In the abstraction of some philosopher, this might seem fair, but I do not know anyone who suggests a system where Bill Gates and an impoverished adult would owe the same in taxes. Bill Gates can afford to pay a great deal more in taxes and still maintain a very good lifestyle and so our tax system is, at least in theory, designed to make Gates pay more. Now there are many who advocate a flat tax, but most of these people say that not everyone should be taxed. Steve Forbes, who advocated such a tax, proposed that it would begin with those making $40,000 a year. Even if this flat tax were applied to every cent of earnings, Bill Gates would pay much more tax than any of us. Mill concludes that we base our tax system on the public good. Taken as a whole it is better for everyone if the rich pay more and many of the rich seem to agree. Bill Gates needs an educated public to buy his operating systems. His company cannot function if the nation is not secure or if there is great social unrest. He has an interest in maintaining the social structure of the United States and the world. It is better for everyone if those who can afford to pay more do pay more. It is questionable whether the rich do pay more in the United States. In a recent study of the U.S. tax code, David Cay Johnston suggests that the burden of taxes falls unduly on those making between $50,000 and $500,000 a year. Those who make more than $500,000 hire tax lawyers who find loopholes in the tax laws. Some of these lawyers and lobbyists have so much influence that they even write parts of the tax laws. Corporations are also adept at creating tax loopholes. Enron, to name one infamous example, paid no taxes for several years before its demise, even as it was reporting great profits. It is hard to say what is fair in the questions of taxation. It is also difficult to ensure that practice matches our theory of justice. Johnston quotes a prominent tax attorney who said that no member of Congress has had a comprehensive understanding of the U.S. tax system since Wilbur Mills, and Mills left Congress in 1977. Johnston argues that when all taxes are considered—income, social security, sales taxes, and estate taxes—the rate that the poor are paying seems about the same as the rate on the wealthiest 1 percent of Americans (to be in this group you had to have an adjusted gross income of more than $313,000), but the rich have many ways to hide their income so that in fact they are paying taxes at a lower rate than the poor. In the years ahead, as more and more of the wealthy learn to exploit tax loopholes, Johnston predicts that the super-rich will pay even less.

Mill's point about the ethics of taxation is well taken. Utility is a key factor in determining the fairness of taxation. Johnston's book shows us the importance of diving into the details of the situation in order to understand the outcomes that the ethical principles actually produce. See John Stewart Mill *Utilitarianism* (Hackett: Indianapolis, 2002). David Cay Johnston *Perfectly Legal: The Covert Campaign to Rig Our Tax System to Benefit the Super Rich—And Cheat Everybody Else* (New York: Portfolio, 2003).

46. See *Theaetetus* 174a. I have used Seth Benardete's translation *Plato's Theaetetus* (Chicago: The University of Chicago Press, 1986)
47. Aristotle *The Politics* 1259a1 ff

Chapter Two

The Luck of Our Draw

Much of what even the relatively affluent buy is frivolous and the needs of the poor are great. The extremes of poverty and wealth are so pronounced. There really is something obscene about the fact that many of us who are moderately wealthy do not give very much to help alleviate this desperate poverty. It does not seem very difficult to see the right thing to do. Some of the people in this world have a great deal, but most are desperately poor.[1] Almost half of the world's population lives on $2.00 or less a day. How many philosophers does it take to see that we who spend money frivolously have an obligation to give to the poor?

The English word "charity" comes from the Latin word "charitas" and has often been used to translate the New Testament Greek word "agape." As such, the word "charity" has long been associated with "selfless giving." For example, the King James version of the Bible uses the word "charity" in translating Paul's well-known passage 1 Corinthians 13:13 "But now abideth faith, hope, and charity, these three, but the greatest of these is charity." In other translations, charity is replaced with love, but the connection between "charity" and agape is instructive. Charity is thought to be selfless love. Charity is the giving that Christ taught that demands nothing in return. But is our charity really such a selfless act? Or is the concept of charity used to cover (since we have invoked Paul, let us use theological language) a multitude of sins? Is giving to the poor really an act of charity, i.e., selfless giving, or is it something the privileged owe to those who have not had the advantages of birth—advantages that we consciously or unconsciously have come to believe are our birthrights?

I am not against giving money to relieve poverty, but charity—with its undertones of agape—is only one and probably not the most important thing we need to do in addressing the ethical problems associated with poverty. It is true that many of us who are wealthy should probably give more than we do. More importantly, as I will address in the next chapter, those of us who are wealthy—and remember I am thinking of wealth in a global context where even middle-class people in the United States, and increasingly the middle class in the developing world should be considered wealthy—should also work to reform the systems that privilege the wealthy. The history of colonialism and the structure of international trade are only two of the systemic factors that have often favored the wealthy at the expense of the poor. Both within countries and in the relations between countries, the interests of the poor, and even the interests of the middle class are often trampled. Giving of our wealth is one way that those of us who have benefited from these injustices can give to those who have not.

All too often, we do not reflect upon the ways in which we are privileged. A friend of mine, working in advertising, once met a very wealthy and prominent man—a man who is, in fact, mentioned in this book—who in a moment of both humor and candor offered to share the secret of his success. He confessed the secret was "inheritance." Of course, there are other stories. Some have made their money with considerably less help from their families. I have not received millions in inheritance, but I was born to a middle class family in the wealthiest nation on earth. I have worked hard, at times, but have rarely worked the twelve hour days of manual labor that I have seen many Africans work. I have benefited from government programs such as student loans and have received my education in well-funded public schools from kindergarten through the completion of my undergraduate degree. And my parents also had the opportunity to attend excellent public schools in the United States at a time when most African Americans and many others were systematically excluded. For that matter, as I was attending fine public schools in the 1960s and early 1970s, there were not many African Americans, not to mention the global poor, who had that opportunity. Indeed, most Americans did not have schools as good as mine. Some wealthy people have made their money by overcoming enormous difficulties, but the accumulation and retention of wealth does not rely solely or even principally on individual effort. When Bill Gates and Warren Buffett argue for the inheritance tax they do so because their accumulation of wealth was only possible in a land where citizens are educated and in good health. They believe that the accident of birth should not be the determining factor of a child's fate. Warren Buffett and for that matter the great champion of free markets, Milton Friedman, have explicitly acknowledged the role of luck in their successes. By paying inheritance taxes, Gates and Buffett are giving back to the country that made their vast fortunes possible. No one makes it all by themselves. Some are born with great intelligence. Some are born into upper-middle-class suburbs with good schools and stable homes—most of the world is born into poverty.

Liberals can sometimes be too quick to criticize the government for all failings in society. Cornel West, for one, has pointed out that individual responsibility cannot be ignored, but he also argues eloquently that those who have been the beneficiaries of systemic imbalances have an ethical obligation to help open the system for others.[2] Even within the United States it is obvious that everyone does not have an equal chance at success. Too often in the United States people who have been given very little opportunity to succeed are criticized for failing. According to the most recent U.S. census figures, more than 37 percent of all African American children in the United States live in what the government itself defines as poverty. And most agree that the way poverty is calculated by the United States census undercounts the actual number. These children clearly do not have the same chance of gaining the education that is crucial to their economic success as the children of the middle class. And most of the children born in the poor nations of Africa—many of whom will die in infancy—have even a lesser chance of escaping poverty. Those of us who have been born into relative affluence, have had the opportunity to attend good schools, have had good health care, have never had to think twice about where to find clean water and always had a roof over our heads have had opportunities that are denied to many of the poor. Not all of us live off an inheritance, but many of us have been well-placed by the accident of our birth to live lives of relative affluence. Many more have been born into poverty the overcoming of which demands labors scarcely less daunting than those of Hercules.

Many of the poor in the United States as well as the poor in other lands are working to make my life possible. Even if someone is not directly involved in contributing to our lives, this does not mean that we have no ethical responsibility to them. Some of the poor are so marginalized that they have not found a place in the United States' or world economies. I will argue that we have ethical responsibilities to these people as well, particularly those of us who have been given so many opportunities to succeed.

THE ADVANTAGES OF BIRTH

Blaming the poor for their poverty is a time-honored tactic and very widespread. For example, in the 1870s the *Japanese Gazette*, an English-language newspaper published in Japan, reported that Japan would never become wealthy because the "love of indolence and pleasure of the people themselves forbid it." The paper went on to suggest that principles of the West, when transferred to the East "tend fatally towards weediness and corruption."[3] Today we often hear that poverty is simply the result of a lack of individual initiative or that poverty stems from the moral failings of the poor. As Patricia Hill Collins and Ama Aidoo argue, there are many images in the media that suggest that African women "breed" too many children and expect the world to pick up the tab. Not only are these women portrayed surrounded by children, suggesting that they are sexually irresponsible, they are also often portrayed with a begging bowl in their hands and "seen as too far gone to be worthy of aid or as passive recipients of government handouts."[4] Similarly, black women in the United States are seen as responsible for the poverty of their children by virtue of their sexuality and are also seen as impossible to help. In the United States, women of color are often blamed (explicitly or implicitly) for not controlling their fertility (even while the rate of pregnancy among teenage African Americans has been declining), but rarely do individuals hold themselves responsible for not giving young girls and boys the education and economic security that will enable them to control their fertility.[5] Individual comportment should play a role in judging one's action for both the poor and the rich, but who we are and our actions are also influenced by economic and social structures.[6] The poor are often faulted for lack of initiative, while even the relatively affluent deny their own failure to provide opportunities for the poor to succeed. Why are the wealthy not judged for not having helped to provide the resources that the poor need such as education and health care?

We live in a world, and those of us living in the United States live in a nation, of brutal inequalities and we have learned to live with these inequalities and to ignore the many ways that we benefit from the current economic structure. In hindsight, it is easy to see, to name one example, the self-serving nature of many of the pro-slavery justifications. It is harder to see what lies behind our own moral compass. How often do our moral systems seduce us and merely justify our privilege?

Even those of us who are aware of the world's poverty have learned to live with our awareness. We consume, we blame the victim, and we view the problem as too big to fix.

Many ask, given that someone has earned his or her money fairly, do they really have a moral obligation to give it away? Who has earned their money fairly? Is it not the case that many of us have been groomed to succeed while others have been prepared for failure? And, if this is true, how much stronger the argument is for giving back a modest percentage of what we earned with the help of our educational and other advantages! Herbert A. Simon, a Nobel Prize–winning economist, has estimated that limited access to social capital, rather than wealth, is the principle cause of poverty. Some begin their lives in Somalia and others in Europe or North America. Simon estimates that 90 percent of our wealth in Europe and the United States is due to the accident of our birth.[7]

In the United States, there are many who lack access to social capital, as even a brief examination of our educational system shows. Jonathan Kozol has been documenting the failures of the U.S. educational system for more than thirty years. His book *Savage Inequalities* remains, even though it was written more than twenty years ago, one of the most eloquent and incisive indictments of inequality in the United States that I have ever read, and there is little evidence that the conditions that the book describes have changed much since it was written.[8] *Savage Inequalities*, opens with a deeply disturbing account of East St. Louis, a river town, bordered on the west by the Mississippi River and surrounded on the east by bluffs, on which predominately white, relatively wealthy towns have been built. The water that flows from the towns on the bluffs down onto East St. Louis contributes to the problems of East St. Louis, for one of its greatest problems is the lack of a functioning sewer system. The towns on the bluffs pay nothing to help solve the problems that their water runoff helps to create. Kozol quotes a professor of public policy who says that physical separation "helps to rationalize the psychological and cultural distance that those on the Bluffs have clearly tried to maintain."[9] Poverty is much easier to accept when it is hidden. One of the great services that Kozol and others provide is that they make poverty visible.

Kozol's descriptions of East St. Louis are particularly poignant. East St. Louis has been called the most distressed small city in America. It has the highest fetal death rate and the highest premature birth rate in Illinois. It is heavily polluted by chemical plants and a hazardous waste incinerator. In most inner cities, one worries about the paint containing lead in old buildings. In East St. Louis there are high concentrations of lead in the soil because of the plants that incinerate hazardous wastes and produce chemicals in the town. Lead poisoning is a particularly insidious health hazard, given that it causes irreparable brain damage.

The schools of East St. Louis are in desperate shape. For example, almost all of the schools had to be shut down when sewage flowed into one of the school's kitchens. Since the kitchen provided meals for the entire district, most of the district's children were unable to attend school.[10] The buildings are old and crumbling. Heating systems do not work, books are lacking, and the district saves money by hiring "substitute" teachers that earn $10,000 a year. The city has the highest property tax rate in the state, but there is not much property to tax. The chemical plants that have contributed so much pollution escape city taxes by incorporating themselves into towns. Furthermore, the tax revenues that are collected are used up trying to maintain buildings that are plagued with a number of problems, such as inefficient heating systems and poor insulation. Lack of money may not be the only problem in the schools of East St. Louis, but it is a massive problem.

It is hard to overestimate our proclivity to separate ourselves, emotionally and physically, from poverty. Once when I was teaching the book, a student raised his hand and said that he was convinced that Kozol was making it up. By some miracle of fate another student raised her hand and said that she had spent the last two summers doing missionary work in the city and it was every bit as bad as Kozol claimed. East St. Louis was literally left off the map of Illinois at one point and its residential and business telephone numbers were left out of the telephone directory.[11] But our ability to wall off poverty does not need natural borders, such as rivers and bluffs. Kozol also writes about disparities within cities—even disparities between communities that lie right next to each other. In Chicago, he writes of a new housing development populated by middle- and upper-middle-class parents who were able to convince the school board to build a new school in their neighborhood and effectively block children from adjoining lower-class neighborhoods from attending. Kozol also tells about how in New York City, within a single school district there are vastly different schools. He visits one school that is housed in a former skating rink. Most of its classrooms have no windows and many classes have to share rooms. In some rooms there are as many as four different classes meeting with little to separate them. This school is supposed to hold 900 students, but in fact has more than 1,300. Classes are supposed to be no larger than thirty-four, but Kozol sees one with thirty-seven. The school library has about seven hundred books and there are twenty-six computers for the entire school. The children have, at most, two gym classes per week and have no place to have recess. The school is 90 percent black and Hispanic

In the very same district, there is another school that serves the wealthy and predominately white neighborhood of Riverdale. It has 825 children, but has a library of almost eight thousand books. It has a playground with state-of-the-art play structures. The classes Kozol sees have twenty-two or twenty-three students and lots of windows. The school in the skating rink has no encyclopedias in the library and none in the classrooms. The school in Riverdale has a recent set in every classroom. It is not only the school district that allocates unequally. Kozol reports that the state legislature also gives disproportionately to rich districts; "the poorest districts in the city get approximately 90 cents per pupil from legislative grants (i.e., grants given by state legislators) while the richest districts have been given $14 for each pupil."[12]

One student says:

> We have a school in East St. Louis named for Dr. King . . . The school is full of sewer water and the doors are locked with chains. Every student in that school is black. It's a terrible joke on history.[13]

The girl is pointing out the irony of naming segregated schools after the man who dreamed of black and white children walking hand in hand to school. Kozol points out that Riverdale is a politically liberal district. Whites from Riverdale went south to protest racial discrimination during the 1960s. Kozol speculates that it is not that the wealthy, predominately white parents of

Riverdale want the poor children of District 10 to be harmed, but "they simply want the best for their own children."[14]

In the more than twenty years since Kozol wrote *Savage Inequalities* the problems have not gone away. In 2004, the *New York Times* cited a report from the Education Trust, a nonpartisan group that represents poor urban schools, that New York State has the greatest disparities in state funding for education. "The poorest students receive $2,152 per student less from state and local government sources than schools with the fewest needy students."[15] New York City has sued the state of New York for underfunding its schools and the courts have found in the city's favor. Similar lawsuits have been brought in other states as well. In a more recent book, *The Shame of a Nation: The Restoration of Apartheid Schooling in America*, Kozol documents how little has changed in the years since he wrote *Savage Inequalities*, even as the United States has supposedly committed itself to "leaving no child behind." In this more recent book, Kozol cites figures, again compiled by the Education Trust, that show that a typical class of twenty-five low-income children in Texas receives $23,000 less than a class of twenty-five children who are not poor. In Virginia, the difference between the two classrooms is $36,000, and in New York State where the difference is the greatest, it is $65,000. The differences grow even greater in many states if you examine the funding gap for minority students. The funding gap between classes of minority students and majority students in California is twice as large as the gap for low income children.[16] The funding gap between wealthy schools and poor schools is even larger. In 2003, Manhasset, a wealthy suburb of New York, spent almost twice as much per child on education as New York City—a ratio that was almost exactly the same as in 1987.

Kozol argues that the United States simply accepts the notion that poor children will receive less of an education in the United States than wealthy children. The problem is not that wealthy children receive too much, but that poor children do not receive enough and taxpayers do not seem prepared to pay more in taxes to improve education for poor children.

Studies show, not surprisingly, that the United States' top colleges are increasingly being populated by the children of wealthy parents. In 1985, 46.1 percent of the students in the top 250 colleges and universities were from the top 25 percent of wealthy families. By 2000, 54.9 percent of the students came from the top 25 percent of wealthiest families.[17] "At the most selective private universities in the United States there are more children of doctors than there are children of hourly workers, teachers, clergy members, farmers or members of the military combined." I teach at a fine state liberal arts college and often do an informal, voluntary (obviously confidential) survey of family income of my students. Typically, the average family income in my classes is reported (by the students) to be more than $120,000. We have long known that college education is a good predictor of earning power; now we should recognize that admission to college—even many state universities—is increasingly reserved for the children of the wealthy.

This debate about educational funding shows how inadequate it is to frame our discussion of poverty in terms of charity. In many ways the paths to poverty and wealth are determined by birth and the public policy of our governments. Given that public education in the United States is funded primarily by local property taxes, it should not surprise anyone that the poor receive inferior schools. The solutions to poverty do not lie principally in the charity of the wealthy, but rather in the changing of public policy so that the accident of birth does not play such a large role in determining our economic fate.

Even Marie Antoinette, if one believes the legend, knew that the poor should eat. The legend suggests that she was oblivious to the misery of the poor—and so out of touch with the reality of preparing a daily meal—that she didn't know that cake and bread both require wheat. Most people would agree that the economic system should not be structured in such a way that traps the poor at the bottom and makes them the servants of the wealthy. A healthy dose of blaming the victims has helped us to live with inequalities which many of us, if we think about it long enough, would find morally objectionable. Blaming the poor for their poverty is akin to the self-serving naiveté attributed to Marie Antoinette.

Barbara Ehrenreich calls the poor of America—and I think we could extend her argument to many of the world's poor—the great philanthropists of our time. The working poor are the ones who cook our food, care for our children and our aging parents, sew our clothes, clean our houses, and manufacture our gadgets. Their children are likely to attend poorly equipped and overcrowded schools that will not prepare them for entrance into college. Poor children are often neglected by their own families while the parents work low paying jobs to help care for the families of the rich. We, the wealthy, may feel that charity should begin at home, not realizing that the homes where charity begins are often the substandard housing of the working poor.

Given the educational advantages of the wealthy and the upper middle class we can see that the wealthy's charitable contributions are a small price to pay for the sustained economic advantages that have helped propel them to their places of privilege. As I will argue in more detail in the next chapter, more important than charity is to work to change the systems so that many more have a chance to succeed.

MUST THE POOR ALWAYS BE WITH US?

The giving of money is not the most important part of responding to poverty. I have emphasized the poverty that exists in both the United States and the world, and given our ability to overlook poverty—even poverty in our midst—I believe I am right to do so, but we should not overlook the progress that has been made in combating poverty. The World Bank reports that in developing countries over the last twenty years life expectancy at birth has increased by twenty years, illiteracy has been cut in half, and even though the world's population has increased by 1.6 billion the number of poor has declined by 200 million. Recent history has shown us that poverty can be greatly reduced.

Successful development is not primarily the result of foreign aid. In 2000, there was approximately $54 billion given worldwide in foreign aid while direct foreign investment in the developing countries was $167 billion. Successful development begins with the developing countries themselves—Korea, Singapore, and China attest to that. Foreign aid is a small part of the picture. Wealthy nations should increase foreign aid, but as we will see in the next chapter, there are even more important things that wealthy nations should do to promote development, for example, wealthy countries also need to lower their trade barriers and lower their agricultural subsidies. As we will see, this will often help not only the poor in the global south, but also the middle class.

Framing the issue in terms of charity can serve to obscure the privilege of the wealthy, but failure to reflect on the responsibility for giving is to let wealthy nations and individuals off the hook too easily. Direct giving is often not what countries or individuals need. The World Bank stresses that countries, particularly those at the early stages of development, often need help with analysis, advice, and capacity building more than money. Nonetheless, at some point, financial assistance is warranted and this raises questions. How much should we as individuals give and how much should we as a nation give?

The United Nations has set a goal to eradicate extreme poverty and hunger in the world. By 2015, it aims to reduce by half the number of people living on less than a dollar a day, as well as halve the number of people who do not have access to clean drinking water.[18] More specifically, the Millennium Report has eight goals: achieve universal primary education; promote gender equality and empower women; reduce child mortality; improve maternal health; combat HIV/AIDS, malaria and other diseases; ensure environmental sustainability; and develop open trading and financial systems that are rule based, predictable, and nondiscriminatory.[19] Almost everyone would agree that these are laudable goals, but some question whether we know how to achieve them. To accomplish this will take, among other things, money. To fulfill these goals, a new report estimated that the wealthy nations of the world need to raise their levels of giving to one-half of 1 percent of their GNP. To do so would require the United States to more than quadruple its foreign aid. The report argues that there are many things that could be done right now, including mass distribution of insecticide-treated bed nets to stop the spread of malaria, elimination of fees for primary education, expansion of school lunch programs, distribution of deworming medicines to school children and expanded AIDS and tuberculosis treatment.[20] Philosophers are clearly not the only ones with grandiose visions! Jeffery Sachs, the chief author of the report, has been heavily criticized for some of the work that he has done with developing nations in the past and there are some who criticize his current work with the Millennium Villages Project.[21] He may overestimate, for example, the effectiveness of his work, but, at the very least, we should applaud his work in drawing attention to the problems and suggesting solutions. No one has all of the answers, but he has some.

Is there any reason to think that we can achieve the Millennium Development Goals? There is no reason to spend money or expend effort in a hopeless cause. The World Bank addresses this issue directly in a paper entitled "The Role and Effectiveness of Development Assistance: Lessons from World Bank Assistance."[22] The paper stresses that economic assistance is only one of a number of steps that can be taken to improve the lot of the world's poor, but the study argues that foreign aid "is an increasingly effective tool for reducing poverty."[23] Life expectancy, literacy, and income have all been improving and past economic aid has had a role in this improvement. The report cites many cases of successful development projects. Public-private partnerships have led to improved literacy rates in Brazil, the complete elimination of smallpox, and sharp reductions of river blindness in West Africa. Bangladesh has cut its infant mortality rate in half and reduced its birth rate by more than half. Again, everyone agrees that these successes are not the result of foreign aid alone—foreign aid is not even the most important part of these successes, but direct assistance is part of the solution. In particular, it seems that foreign aid can help countries that are emerging from civil wars or countries where corrupt regimes have been replaced by governments dedicated to reform.[24]

There have been a number of criticisms of foreign aid recently and some of them have come from World Bank insiders.[25] International organizations are going to great lengths to see what works and there is evidence that institutions are doing a better job of providing development assistance. The World Bank Report estimates that in 1990 the countries with the worst economic policies and institutions were actually receiving more of its development aid than those with better policies. Today, it believes that countries with better policies are receiving more aid than those with less progressive policies and, as a result, aid was nearly three times more effective in 1997 than it was in 1990.[26] Unfortunately, at the same time that aid is becoming more effective, the amount of aid given is dropping.

The World Bank is making a major effort to evaluate the results of its programs. The Bank is being encouraged to conduct randomized trials similar to the randomized trials used by drug companies to test new drugs. In other words, people should be randomly assigned to anti-poverty programs and then their success should be measured against a control group who did not receive the help. A group of development economists from the Massachusetts Institute of Technology has formed an organization named the Abdul Latif Jameel Poverty Action Lab. They argue that randomized trials have been at the heart of medical advances and will be of great benefit in directing foreign aid to programs that really work. The Poverty Action Lab is a network of professors from around the world. It works with NGOs and governments to help scale up highly successful programs. I particularly admire the fact that they have four regional offices associated with universities in Africa, Europe, Latin America and South Asia. Building capacity in a country seems to me to be one of the most valuable services that an organization like this can offer.

Showing that a program really works should also encourage donors to give more.[27] For example, a study of Kenyan schoolchildren showed that giving drugs for intestinal worms was a more cost-effective way of keeping them in school than providing these students with a free breakfast or free school uniforms. Another program in Mexico, Oportunidades, which pays poor mothers a small sum if they immunize their children and keep them in school, has also been shown, in a randomized trial, to be effective.[28] Documenting the success of the Mexican program has led to its being adopted across Latin America, most notably in Brazil. Brazil is one of the few countries in the world right now where inequality has been decreasing. The country stands as a model for poverty reduction. It is important to note, however, that these programs are not paid for by international donors, but by the governments themselves.[29]

One program that is supported by international donors and is receiving positive attention is the Global Fund to Fight AIDS, Tuberculosis, and Malaria. This program is a public/private partnership. It was developed with contributions from a number of parties including the United States, Italy, the World Bank, WHO, UNICEF, and the Islamic Development Bank, as well as with contributions from private aid organizations, foundations, the private sector countries themselves. Thanks to this coordinated effort the number of cases of malaria in Senegal dropped from 300,000 in 2008 to 175,000 in 2009. In 2006, there were 400,000 cases of malaria in children under five (malaria is particularly dangerous for young children) in Senegal, by 2009, that number had dropped to 30,000 confirmed cases.[30]

In the *Encyclopedia* of Diderot and D'Alembert, the distinction is made between the empirical doctor who decides each case individually and the rational doctor who uses the light of reason to determine treatment. Medical practice has a long tradition of believing that it is guided by reason. But a case could be made that much of medical practice is, in fact, guided by tradition. Evaluating social programs presents even greater challenges than the evaluation of medical practices because social conditions vary much more widely than biological factors. Knowing that a poverty reduction program works in Africa may not tell us much about whether or not it would work in Asia. Knowing that it works in one part of Africa, or one part of a particular country, may not tell us much about whether it will work in another part of Africa. The World Bank stresses the need to work with local governments in order to tailor programs to local needs.

The United States is a notoriously cheap nation when it comes to foreign aid.[31] Even though George W. Bush increased the amount of foreign aid that the United States gives, we as a nation are giving approximately .15 percent of GNP in foreign aid. The United Nations has proposed that nations give 0.7 percent of GNP in foreign aid and Denmark, the Netherlands, Luxembourg, and Sweden actually have exceeded that goal. To give at the recommended levels the United States would have to give almost five times what it gives now. The small amount that we give appears even more miserly when we consider who gets the aid. For the most part, we give the aid to those with whom we are trying to court favor. In the last few years the top aid recipients have typically been Iraq, Afghanistan, Egypt, Pakistan, and Colombia—all nations from whom we are seeking political favors. So not only should we give aid, we should give it to nations that will use it wisely. The devil is often in the details. In the midst of the debate about how to reduce the deficit in the United States, some have proposed reducing or even eliminating foreign aid. This is, according to the public opinion polls, one of the few deficit-reducing measures that has wide scale public support. Of course many in the United States do not realize how little foreign aid the United States gives. A recent Kaiser Family Foundation survey showed that, on average, Americans thought that 28 percent of the United States' government budget went to foreign aid when in fact foreign aid represents less than 1 percent of government spending.[32] Cutting or even eliminating foreign aid would not come even close to solving the deficit, but it will result in many preventable deaths.

It is also important to note that promises of aid do not equal aid delivered. There was a dramatic outpouring in 2005 in response to the tsunami disaster in Asia, but there were also stories about how previous disaster aid promised by governments never materialized. In October of 1998, Hurricane Mitch killed more than ten thousand people in Honduras, Nicaragua, Guatemala, and El Salvador and caused $9 billion in property damage. The world promised $9 billion to rebuild, but most of the money never materialized.[33] Similarly, in Iran, only $17 million of the $1 billion dollars pledged to help rebuild the city of Bam that was destroyed by an earthquake on December 26, 2003, has been delivered. Sometimes, tragically, aid is not even promised. The 2010 floods in Pakistan affected more than 20 million people, more people than were affected by the Asian tsunami, Hurricane Katrina and the Haitian earthquake combined, and yet contributions were slow in coming.

As citizens we clearly should lobby our governments to give more, as well as hold our governments accountable for the promises they do make. We should work to ensure the money is spent wisely and does not merely flow into the hands of corrupt officials that do our bidding. But we should not just rely on the government.

A VERY MODEST PROPOSAL

We, as individuals, should do more as well, particularly those of us who have disposable income, to alleviate poverty. According to Peter Unger, a $250 contribution to an aid agency such as CARE or Oxfam can save the life of a child. There are 1.9 million deaths, mostly infants and young children, every year from dehydration.[34] Children under two are particularly susceptible. Given that 1.2 billion people do not have access to clean drinking water, and two billion do not have access to sewage systems, diarrheal diseases are rampant. Young children without access to clean drinking water are particularly susceptible to diarrhea and subsequent dehydration. Oral rehydration packets cost less than a dollar and are very effective in saving lives. These aid agencies have large overhead costs so one must assume that the cost of delivering these services will be high, but Unger believes that $250 per life saved is a reasonable estimate.

If we want to educate the children we save, this can also be done, in many cases for what is to Westerners very little money. Schools in the developing world often have what seem, in the West, very nominal fees. In the United States there are many upper-middle-class parents who put their children in private schools out of concern (a concern which may be justified, but perhaps is not) about the quality of the public schools. In developing countries there are many children who cannot afford even the minimal fees that public schools charge. In Guatemala, for example, school fees and uniforms can cost $250. In Kenya, the elimination of the $17-a-year school fees led to large increases in the number of students attending public schools. Education is important not only for the child being educated. Education of the mother is the single greatest predictor for the survival of children. Is it right to pay $20,000 a year to put one's child in private school in the United States when that same $20,000 would pay for eighty children to go to school in Guatemala? Good news here—many who send their children to private schools could afford to pay tuition and give a substantial amount to charity as well. Friends of mine gave $250 a year for six years to keep a Guatemalan girl in school. She graduated at the top of her class and attended medical school in Cuba.

Philosophers have long debated about whether we should help family and friends before we help strangers. We have debated about the moral significance of political borders. There may well be good reasons to help family and friends first, but one could also make an argument that we should pay close attention to those most in need. The decision to bring children into the world does imply the obligation to care for them. Given the tendency in the United States, in particular, to curb social programs, one is unable to count on the government to care for loved ones. Similarly, one can reasonably be expected to care for one's parents if they have cared for you. There is also an argument to be made for caring for one's self. Failure to save money for retirement, for example, could lead one to need charity from others.

Parents have an obligation to their own children, but don't all of us who have money have an obligation to the very poor? Most of us are in a position to both care for ourselves and for our families, and still give to others. As I have said before, there are good reasons to be suspicious of moral crusades that ask us to make great sacrifices for a cause. The fact that many of us have a great deal of discretionary income means that we should be able to pay our share toward the reduction of extreme poverty without even coming close to sacrificing something of great importance!

To help us think about how much we should give, Singer writes about the distinction between giving until we sacrifice something of moral importance and giving until we sacrifice something of equal moral importance. To sacrifice something of moral importance means sacrificing something that really makes a difference in our lives. We do not have to sacrifice, for example, our own food, or health care or shelter, but we should sacrifice our luxuries so that others will have the basic necessities needed to survive. Even though I truly love a good meal, I must admit that going out to a "nice restaurant" is a luxury that is far from essential. To give until we sacrifice something of comparable moral significance is a higher standard. This standard suggests that we should give until we have impoverished ourselves to the same level as those who need our help.

There are good reasons for discounting the second, stricter standard. As Singer points out, giving to a point where we impoverish ourselves may severely limit our ability to give in the future. If one sells one's car and gives the money to those who cannot afford a car, for example, one may lose one's job and one's ability to earn more money that could help more people. Therefore, giving all of one's resources until one is reduced to poverty in order to help the poor may leave the poor, in the long run, less well-off. Even if this standard of giving to the point of poverty does not make much sense, within Singer's utilitarian perspective, it is interesting to note that it has been followed by some. The renunciation of worldly wealth is, after all, the story of the Buddha. St. Francis of Assisi is another famous example of one who gave away all earthly possessions. After his conversion, St. Francis vowed never to sleep inside and to wear only clothes made out of material discarded by others. If nothing else, those who renounce all worldly possessions remind us that some of the great wise people of the world have often eschewed worldly goods. And even if their eschewing of all earthly goods leaves them little to give to others, their example has motivated others.

As time goes on, Singer is becoming, in some respects, less demanding. He is no longer even asking most of us to give according to the lesser standard. In *Practical Ethics,* Singer suggests giving 10 percent of one's income to help the poor of the world.[35] He notes that this is an arbitrary figure. Some will be able to give more and some will give less, but for most of the relatively affluent Singer argues that the 10 percent standard "by any reasonable ethical standard . . . is the minimum we ought to do, and we do wrong if we do less." In *One World*, he suggests that everyone give 1 percent toward the elimination of global poverty.[36] He seems to be lowering the bar because he is afraid that by asking people to give more, they may end up deciding to give nothing at all. He believes that the 1 percent donation is the minimal and not the optimal standard. Those who think seriously about their obligations will give more, but Singer is concerned about success—changing the world—and he thinks that many can be persuaded to give 1 percent. Singer speculates that giving 1 percent would provide more than double what the United Nations says is needed for the Millennium Goals and might lead to the elimination of poverty—not just the reduction by half. He is perhaps overly optimistic. Political will, in the wealthy nations as well as the poor nations, is needed as well as money. But anti-poverty efforts have not yet reached the point where they have too much money.

In his most recent work Singer suggests a sliding scale and demands more of the very wealthy.[37] Those at the very top income levels—averaging more than $10 million in income a year should give a third of their yearly income above $10 million and somewhat less of a percentage of their income below that level. Singer's recommended giving percentage gradually decreases as income decreases until those in the top 10 percent who make at least $105,000 are told they should give at least 5 percent of their income above that amount. If such standards were applied to only U.S. taxpayers Singer estimates that $471 billion could be raised annually for poverty reduction. If the rest of the world contributed its fair share and those making less than $92,000 would contribute 1 percent that would yield $1.5 trillion, which would be more than eight times what Jeffery Sachs estimates it would cost to achieve the Millennium Development Goals. Interestingly, as Singer notes, there is evidence that many people of modest means give substantially more of their income to charity. He cites one study that showed that people making under $20,000 typically give 4.6 percent of their yearly income to charity, which is a higher percentage than those of every other income group below $300,000.[38] Those of us who make more than $20,000 should be inspired by this example.

Singer has often used an argument from analogy to underscore why we should give money to charities that target global poverty. He argues that failure of even the moderately wealthy to give money to alleviate severe poverty is analogous to an adult walking past a child drowning in a small pond because one was reluctant to ruin a new pair of shoes. The analogy underscores how frivolous many of our purchases are when compared to the needs of the world's poorest people. If we knew with certainty that a relatively small contribution to a charity would save a life, then the case for giving to charity would be strong. Recently Leif Wenar has argued that Singer's pond argument is flawed because aid agencies cannot assure us that our contributions actually save lives.[39] Wenar discusses how aid is often ineffective and he argues that it can sometimes even hurt the very people it is trying to help.

Specifically, Wenar lists seven challenges that charitable organizations face. First, when aid is needed quickly, for example, the Haitian earthquake, aid agencies may rush into action and duplicate one another's efforts. On the other hand, major public health problems—such as the AIDS epidemic—need a long-term engagement. Wenar suggests that many NGOs do not develop the in-country relations and expertise that they need to be effective. Second, Wenar worries about the lack of local participation in many aid projects. If governments or communities do not feel "ownership" of these products, it is hard for them to be successful. Third, Wenar fears that there is often diversion of aid resources and if the aid diverted empowers corrupt local officials it can actually make things worse for the poor. As an example of this he cites a study of education aid in Uganda that showed that schools only received, on average, 13 percent of the grants they were given. The rest of the money was siphoned off by corrupt local officials. Interestingly, however, this study does not assess the effectiveness of charitable giving, but rather how effective the Ugandan government was in assuring that grants the government gave for school expenditures, other than teachers' wages, actually went to the schools.[40] Next, Warner worries about the economic effects of aid. Aid agencies often hire some of the best people away from other sectors of a country's economy. Large aid influxes can also inflate a nation's currency. There have been recent reports from Afghanistan that suggest this is a problem there. Fifth, he worries that poorly coordinated aid projects can work against each other. He gives the example of how an aid project that supports refugee camps can work against a project that is trying to resettle the refugees back to their lands. Sixth, aid can break the social contract within a nation. If citizens and political officials become too reliant on foreign aid it diminishes the tie between the citizens and their political leaders. Finally, aid can, by privileging some groups over others, increase the gaps in wealth and power within the poor countries. All of these worries lead Warner to two conclusions. One, it is likely that some aid will make some people worse off, and, two, it is difficult to make a reliable estimate of the overall effects of any individual's contribution.

Singer tries to head off such objections by citing two groups that seek to evaluate the effectiveness of aid. GiveWell is an organization started by former Wall Street hedge fund managers that attempts to evaluate the effectiveness of aid agencies. It evaluates a large number of charitable organizations in an attempt to find a very few of the most effective organizations. It only recommends a small number of charities. Currently it has identified six charities that it considers the most effective NGOs doing international work and four NGOs doing the most effective work in the United States.

Wenar criticizes GiveWell explicitly. He questions GiveWell's and Singer's claims that it is possible to estimate how much it would cost to save a life. To highlight the problems he sees he investigates GiveWell's rating of one NGO in particular, PSI. Wenar quotes a claim that appeared as late as 2009 on GiveWell's website that estimated that if one gave $820 to the charity PSI, one could be "reasonably certain" that one had saved a life. PSI is involved in, among other things, distributing bed nets in Africa in an attempt to reduce malaria and distributing condoms. GiveWell has followed PSI longer than any other organization. Elie Hassenfeld, one of the cofounders of GiveWell, explains that PSI was the recipient of his first substantial donation. In 2007 it was GiveWell's top ranked international NGO and for that it received a $25,000 grant from the organization. In 2009 GiveWell reassessed PSI and its rating dropped from first to fourth on GiveWell's recommended list of most effective international charities. In 2010 GiveWell reassessed again and questioned whether or not PSI programs were really bringing about behavioral changes, i.e., even if bed net usage and condom usage were increasing, was PSI really responsible for this increase. In 2011, GiveWell dropped PSI from its list of the six most effective international NGOs. It gave two reasons for changing its rating. First, GiveWell was concerned about how PSI uses the monitoring data that it collects, and, second, as GiveWell reviewed new data on bed net usage and condom usage from across Africa, it led them to question again whether PSI was actually responsible for increasing bed net and condom usage.[41]

GiveWell does not claim that PSI is not having an impact, but it argues that the new studies on bed net and condom usage in areas not served by PSI means PSI has a new burden of proof to show that its programs are increasing bed net and condom usage. GiveWell says that when it first began the process of evaluating charities, PSI was the only NGO "that seemed to have any meaningful data on its impact."[42] Although it no longer counts PSI as one of its top six international charities, GiveWell praises the organization for its transparency and Hassenfeld estimates that the charity is in the top 1 percent of all international charities in "terms of its impact per dollar."[43]

In addition to being evaluated by GiveWell, PSI is one of the NGOs that have worked with the Poverty Action Lab, an organization that I have already discussed. Both GiveWell and the Poverty Action Lab are trying to study scientifically what strategies work in poverty reduction. We should not be surprised if some of the things that NGOs and governments try do not work. Wenar may well be right about the narrow issue that it is difficult to know exactly if a specific donation actually saved a life. He even seems right to raise questions about the efficacy of GiveWell's early efforts to rate charities. The GiveWell website admits that its methodology for judging the effectiveness of NGOs is evolving. Wenar criticizes GiveWell for not having a good basis for making its original assessments of PSI and GiveWell seems to admit this. But there is evidence that GiveWell, the Poverty Action Lab and other organizations are improving their evaluation tools.

PSI may be more effective than Wenar suggests. It is working with both GiveWell and the Poverty Action Lab to evaluate the effectiveness of its programs. A friend of mine who has worked on malaria eradication for many years and worked with PSI has praised it for its effectiveness. I agree with Wenar that we cannot be sure that our donation will save a life, but there is good reason to give in the hope that our donations will help poor people and contribute to learning more about what works. The analogy to the child drowning in the pond is not perfect—analogies never are, but the analogy does highlight how children are dying and how a small sacrifice on our part might really make a difference. Unlike saving a child drowning in a shallow pond, the circumstances surrounding poverty are complex. As I have already said, at least since Aristotle we have known that ethics is an imprecise endeavor. Good people are making good-faith efforts to improve the effectiveness of aid. Why not get on board and lend our support, particularly if it requires only a very modest sacrifice?

There are times and situations that demand great moral heroism. During the Second World War and the genocide in Rwanda, to name only two examples, people were faced with truly horrible situations and some laid down their lives for others. There is great suffering today—in South Sudan and the Congo, for example—and troops are putting their lives at risk to try to protect civilians. Even if we cannot be sure of exactly how effective our contributions will be, it seems little to ask us to make very modest sacrifices to help the world identify and implement poverty-reduction programs. These programs will not be perfect and many will be poorly thought-out and poorly implemented. We must be careful because many aid organizations may not be doing much good. We should investigate before we give. I applaud the work of GiveWell and the Poverty Action Lab and all those organizations, such as PSI, who are willing to submit themselves to rigorous examination in their efforts to be effective.

It is easy to lampoon the extravagance of the rich. Jerry Seinfeld is reported by *Time* magazine to have not only thirty-six Porsches, but also a three-story garage in Manhattan to store them. Moving down the scale, there are many in the United States who drive luxury cars costing $30,000 or much more. There are very good cars costing thousands of dollars less that offer very good safety, durability, and good repair records. Should anyone be driving a Mercedes or a Lexus when they could drive a Toyota and save the lives of many who live in absolute poverty? Buy a $20,000 Toyota instead of a $35,000 Lexus, and we might be able save fifty children from dying or pay their school costs for one year. Is the comfort of a Lexus worth the life of a child? Or if Wenar is right that we cannot be sure whether we will save a life, is the comfort of a Lexus worth the possibility that one might save the lives of 50 children? Let us go further down the scale: many upper-middle-class people can afford to eat in "nice" restaurants. It is not difficult to spend $125.00 a night in many restaurants and it is possible to spend much more. So for the price of dinner for two at a "fine" restaurant, perhaps I could save a child's life. Even if I cannot be sure that I will save a life, I could at least be sure that I support an organization that is earnestly seeking to help the poor and that is submitting its programs to rigorous evaluations. As Singer has often noted, many of us discard perfectly good clothes and buy new ones merely because we have grown tired of our "old" clothes, or because we feel that our clothes have gone out of style. Is this the right thing to do when almost half the world lives on less than $2.00 a day and there are good organizations that we could support?

The more we think about it, the more absurd these luxuries appear. Most of us living upper-middle-class lives engage in conspicuous consumption—not on the level of Jerry Seinfeld, but conspicuous nonetheless. One could argue that Jerry or those of us who make considerably less than Jerry have earned our money and no one has the right to take it away. But none of the thinkers I have cited are suggesting that we should take Jerry's money or my money. They are arguing that Jerry should freely give up a rather puny part of his luxuries, just as I should freely give up a few of my lesser luxuries. One reason we should do this is because most of us who have disposable income have it, in large measure, by virtue of the luck of our birth. We have had opportunities that most of the world did not and we should help others who have not had the opportunities that we have had. It is not only giving that expects nothing in return, but giving that acknowledges the luck of our draw and the misfortune of many others.

NOTES

1. Richard W. Miller argues that the United States should give more foreign aid, but that it is even more important for the United States to restructure the rules of foreign trade, and modify patent laws and environmental laws. One can lobby for more aid even while one recognizes that this is not the most important thing to do to reduce global poverty. See *Globalizing Justice: The Ethics of Poverty and Power* (Oxford UK: Oxford University Press, 2010) p. 255.

2. See, for example, *Race Matters* (New York: Vintage, 1994) p. 85.

3. As reported in Jeffrey Sach's *The End of Poverty* (Penguin: New York, 2006) 316.

4. Patricia Hill Collins *Black Feminist Thought 2ed.* (New York: Routledge, 2008) 241.

5. Kost K., Henshaw S., and Carlin L., *U.S. Teenage Pregnancies, Births and Abortions: National and State Trends and Trends by Race and Ethnicity*, 2010, http://www.guttmacher.org/pubs/USTPtrends.pdf> accessed Jan. 26, 2010.

6. See Cornel West *Race Matters* (New York: Vintage Books, 1994) 18-19.

7. "UBI and the Flat Tax." Boston Review (Oct./Nov. 2000) http://bostonreview.netBR25.5/simon.html, Branko Milanovic also estimates that much of our wealth is the result of factors beyond our control. He estimates that 80 percent of one's income is determined by the country of one's birth and the income of one's parents. There are also other factors over which people have no control, for example, gender, age, race, and luck.

8. *Savage Inequalities* (New York: Harper Perennial, 1991).

9. Ibid. 9.

10. Ibid. 23.

11. Ibid. 18.

12. *Savage Inequalities* 98.

13. Ibid. 35.

14. Ibid. 108.

15. *The New York Times*, Nov. 9, 2004

16. *Shame of the Nation* (New York: Crown Publishers, 2005) p. 246.

17. *The New York Times*, April 22, 2004.

18. Thomas Pogge has recently argued that these goals have been significantly watered down. See his *Politics as Usual: What Lies Behind the Pro-Poor Rhetoric* (Polity Press: Malden, MA 02148) See especially chapter 2, "The First UN Millennium Goal: A Cause for Celebration?"

19. www.un.org/millenniumgoals

20. For a good summary of the report see "U.N. Proposes Doubling of Aid To Cut Poverty" *New York Times* 1/18/05. For the full report see: http://www.unmillenniumproject.org/documents/MainReportComplete-lowres.pdf

21. See, for example, Nina Munk *The Idealist* (New York: Doubleday, 2013).

22. This paper can be found at http://www.gm-unccd.org/FIELD/Multi/WB/WB_lessons.pdf

23. Ibid. p. ix.

24. See Paul Collier *The Bottom Billion* (Oxford: Oxford University Press, 2008) p. 106 and 115. Cited in Singer *The Life You Can Save* pp.116-7.

25. See Robert Calderisi *The Trouble with Africa: Why Foreign Aid Isn't Working* (New York: Palgrave, 2006) and William Easterly *White Man's Burden: Why the West's Efforts to Aid the Rest Have Done So Much Ill and So Little Good* (New York: Penguin 2006).

26. See the World Bank Report entitled "The Role and Effectiveness of Development Assistance: Lessons from World Bank Assistance" http://www.gm-unccd.org/FIELD/Multi/WB/WB_lessons.pdf

27. Abhijit Banerjee and Esther Duflo *Poor Economics: A Radical Rethinking of the Way to Fight Global Poverty* (Washington, DC: Public Affairs, 2011)

28. See "World Bank Challenged: Are the Poor Really Helped?" *The New York Times* 7/28/04.

29. See "To Beat Back Poverty, Pay the Poor," *The New York Times Opinionator, 1/3/11.*

30. See the Global Malaria Partnership website: http://www.rollbackmalaria.org/ProgressImpactSeries/report4.html

31. These statistics are available from many sources. I am drawing heavily on Peter Singer's *President of Good and Evil: Questioning the Ethics of George W. Bush* (New York: Plume, 2004) pages 122-123.

32. http://kff.org/global-health-policy/poll-finding/2013-survey-of-americans-on-the-u-s-role-in-global-health/

33. *The New York Times* 1/11/05.

34. Howard Markel in *The New York Times*, 30 April 2003, page A31.

35. *Practical Ethics*, 246.

36. *One World*, 193.

37. *The Life You Can Save: Acting Now to End World Poverty* (New York: Random House, 2009) pp. 162-168.

38. Arthur Brooks "The Poor Give More" www.CondeNastPortfolio.com, March 2008, citing the 2000 Social Capital Community Benchmark Survey. I learned of this study from Singer's *The Life You Can Save* p. 166.

39. Leif Wenar "Poverty Is No Pond," in Patricia Illingworth, Thomas Pogge and Leif Wenar, eds, *Giving Well: The Ethics of Philanthropy* (Oxford: Oxford University Press, 2011)

40. Ritva Reinikka and Jakob Svensson, "Local Capture and the Political Economy of School Financing," *Quarterly Journal of Economics* 119 (2004), pp. 679-705. Cited by Wenar in "Poverty Is No Pond."

41. http://blog.givewell.org/2011/04/22/psis-ratings-change/ (Accessed 3 August 2011)

42. http://blog.givewell.org/2011/04/22/psis-ratings-change/ (Accessed 2 August 2011)

43. See GiveWell's blog post "PSI Rating Change" 22 April 2011 http://blog.givewell.org/2011/04/22/psis-ratings-change/ (Accessed on 3 August 2011).

Chapter Three

Mineral Wealth, International Trade, Fair Trade, and Living Wages

Charity is a small part of my modest proposal to the world's moderately wealthy in light of the widespread poverty of our age. The poor are already giving their share so it is time for the moderately wealthy to step up. Of course by wealthy I don't mean just Jerry Seinfield, but all of us who have comfortable middle- and upper-middle-class lives. But, to say it again, to think of our obligation to others in terms of charity obscures the extent to which the poor are often exploited in order to make even the lives of middle-class people possible. Perhaps most strikingly, much of middle-class daily life is made possible by the exploitation of those who live on top of the minerals we use. To drive our cars and heat and cool our homes, oil, coal, and natural gas are often burned. In the next chapter, we will talk about the environmental costs this entails for people all over the world, but here I will begin by exploring how the people who live near these minerals often suffer.

In addition, the current world economic order privileges wealthy nations at the expense of the poor. Forcing developing countries to accept the free flow of capital, the subsidizing of Western agricultural products (along with import controls) and aggressive advocacy for the interests of large corporations are only three of the most important ways that the current world order unduly privileges wealthy nations, or to be more precise, privileges the well-connected. As a middle-class person with a retirement portfolio, I may benefit from the free flow of capital, but I do not benefit from the agricultural subsidies paid to wealthy U.S. agricultural businesses and I often do not benefit from my government's advocacy for large corporations.

One does not have to look very hard to see the benefits colonial powers accrued from their colonies, not to mention the benefit some have derived from slavery. I will not rehearse that history, but mention it to remind us that by looking only at the way things are today, we ignore the ways that the wealthy often owe their wealth to historical advantages.[1] Leaving out many of the ways in which my forefathers' injustices have served to privilege me, I will suggest some ways that the current structuring of globalization should be reformed. Barbara Ehrenreich is right. Our lives—even middle-class lives the world over—are made possible through the work of the poor: factory workers in China, agricultural workers the world over and retail workers in the United States, to name just a few. Many of the world's poor are receiving benefits from their newfound opportunities to work in factories, but we should work together with these workers to curb the excesses. Given that these poor labor on our behalf, we owe them a living wage. They deserve food, clothing, shelter, health care and leisure time for themselves and their families. Exactly how we go about providing them with this is not always clear, but there are a number of ways we can support the living wage movement.[2]

MINERAL WEALTH

For more than forty years, oil has been extracted from the Niger Delta and the people of the Delta have suffered enormously because of it. More gas is flared in the Niger Delta than anywhere else in the world, and, as a result, the delta produces more greenhouse gases than all of the rest of sub-Saharan Africa combined. The people of the Niger Delta once had a diet rich in fish, but today that fish is gone because of the pollution. The flaring has also led to acid rain and other pollution and this has significantly degraded agriculture in the delta. In addition, because of this pollution, many of the local people suffer from "respiratory problems and partial deafness."[3] Nigerian oil is particularly prized in the United States because it is "light sweet crude," and is therefore easily refined and made into gasoline for our cars. It is also easy to ship this oil to the United States.

This oil is not the only thing causing problems in the Niger Delta. The money gained from this oil has enabled vast amounts of corruption within Nigeria, and this has led to an increase in poverty throughout the country since the late 1990s. As I have already noted, Nigeria has one of the shortest life expectancies in the world—212th out of 223 (2014 est.)—even though it ranks 31st in the world in GNP. I don't owe the people of the Niger Delta— or the people of Nigeria—charity; for every mile I drive my car, I owe them restitution. These people don't need my charity, they need justice. They need to get back a portion of the wealth that is taken from their country daily. Fossil fuels make the life of even the middle class possible, but they rarely bring anything but suffering to those who live on top of them or near them. It is true that the United States gets a small fraction of its oil from Nigeria, but it is a fraction that matters. In 2008 when the world's economy was not in recession, attacks by the Niger Delta Vigilante on a hotel lobby and two police stations in Port Harcourt (a city in the delta) helped push the price of oil to over $100 a barrel.[4] Given China's and India's emergence, oil was in particularly tight supply before the recession of 2008. Some have argued that the world has already reached its peak in oil production. Before the recession, even minor disruptions to Nigerian oil were noticed by world markets. Without Nigerian oil, I, and middle-class people the world over, would be paying much more for gasoline.

Nigeria is far from the only place that people have suffered so that I might fill my tank. The Oriente region of Ecuador was an undeveloped rain forest until oil was found there in the 1960s. Most of the oil extracted from this field has gone to California. The oil fields were developed by Texaco, which has since merged with Chevron. Today the area is, by all accounts, an environmental disaster. One of the main problems is that water is pumped into oil wells to force out the crude. The resulting by-product is called "produced water" which is a combination that includes oil, salt, and often metals such as benzene, chromium 6, and mercury.[5] Today it is standard practice to reinject this liquid into the well or to filter out the contaminates. This was also done in some places during the 1970s and 1980s, but not in Ecuador. Environmental activists who are suing Chevron say that more than 18 billion gallons of wastewater and more than 16 million gallons of oil were dumped into either unlined waste pits or directly into Amazonian rivers.

No one disputes that the area has been devastated, but there are vigorous disputes about who is responsible. In 1992, Texaco left Ecuador and the oil extraction was taken over by a state-run company, Petroecudaor, whose environmental record was, by many accounts, not significantly better. Chevron claims that Texaco spent $40 million to clean up the area after it left Ecuador, but activists dispute that the area was properly cleaned and two Chevron lawyers were indicted in Ecuador for their roles in certifying that cleanup had been done. The stakes are very high. The plaintiffs have asked for $113 billion in damages from Chevron.[6] A recent ruling issued by a court in Ecuador assessed a fine of more than $9 billion on Chevron, but the company is vigorously fighting the suit and no one expects it to be settled anytime soon. The people living in the area have been seriously harmed and the area is still an environmental disaster. No one disputes this and that this is wrong. Even Chevron admits that there is serious environmental damage, but they claim they are not the ones who did it.

Chevron has at times been one of the sponsors for Public Broadcasting's Newshour in the United States. The company claims that they are committed to helping Angola develop its oil production in a way that helps the development of the country. Angola is the seventh-largest oil exporter to the United States. Its GDP is the 66th largest in the world and yet it has, according to the

CIA Factbook, one of the world's highest infant mortality rates (eighth high-est in 2014). It also has the world's worst life expectancy (205th in the world in 2014). This is not a poor country, but its oil wealth goes to a small ruling elite that does very little for the vast majority of people living there. Luanda, the capital of Angola, by some estimates, is the world's most expensive city. It was built to house four hundred thousand people, but because many people fled there during the country's civil war, today it is home to more than 3 million people. Most of these people live in slums and, according to the United Nations, somewhere between 80 and 90 percent have no legal claim to their places of residence. Access to drinking water is also a huge problem.[7] Those living in the countryside may be in even worse shape. To be sure, the country's civil war plays a very large role in its current problems. During that war, four million people, almost a quarter of the country's population, were displaced. Land mines left over from the conflict still plague the country and the effort to resettle these displaced people. The war left the system of roads in tatters. Some villages have been cut off from all contact since the end of the civil war. Given that the ruling elite rely on oil revenues to maintain its power it has no pressing need to attend to the needs of its people. Even the IMF, which often rebukes countries for spending too much on social ser-vices, was alarmed by how little money the country was investing in health education, sanitation, and water. The money that is invested in these areas often goes to programs that help only the wealthy. For example, education money goes to scholarships that allow the children of the elite to study at universities in the Europe and the United States. The country has also spent large amounts of money to fly the elite to have their medical treatments in Europe and the United States instead of developing medical services for all in Angola.

It is an unproblematic moral injunction that one should not benefit from stolen goods. Even if one did not steal them, one should not buy them, but all of us who drive cars are benefiting from ill-gotten oil.[8] There is plenty of evidence of theft by the ruling elites in Angola, Nigeria and most other places where oil is extracted. Global Witness reported that between 1997 and 2001, more than $4.2 billion in Angola's national budget went missing. To put this in perspective, this amounted to more than half of Angola's GDP.[9] Some have justified this by saying that Angola was involved in an intense civil war at this time and money was diverted to put an end to it. The civil war ended in 2002, but the problems continue. In December of 2010, Global Witness reported that there was an almost $9 billion gap between oil revenues re-ported by government ministries and what the oil companies reported on their tax reports.[10]

In most places in the world where oil has been found, it has served to make a few fabulously wealthy and lead to the impoverishment of the vast majority. Equatorial Guinea's per capital wealth is equivalent to Spain or

Italy, but more than 77 percent of its citizens live in poverty. There is some evidence to suggest that since the discovery of oil its infant mortality rate has actually risen. In response to the human rights concerns the United States closed its embassy in 1995, but then reopened it largely at the request of Western oil companies who were concerned that Chinese oil companies might gain access to the oil and gas there. Today, the vast majority of the people of Equatorial Guinea suffer, while President Obiang, his family, ExxonMobil, Hess and Marathon grow rich supplying gas to those of us who have automobiles. The son of the president, banks at Wachovia (now Wells Fargo), Bank of America, and USB, has a $35 million estate in Malibu; a $33 million Gulfstream V private jet; and free access to the U.S. even though there is a United States law that is specifically designed to block access to those who have their wealth through raiding their country's coffers. The United States applies those laws to the leaders of Zimbabwe, but Zimbabwe doesn't supply the United States with oil.

Even in the United States, oil extraction has lead companies such as ExxonMobil, ConocoPhillips, and BP to cheat. In Alaska, these companies used a variety of illegal means to increase their profits and ended up settling the court case against them by paying more than $6 billion. In another case, *State of Alabama v. Exxon Mobil Corp*, the state of Alabama was awarded $11.8 billion in punitive damages and $63.6 million in unpaid royalties.[11] As Joseph Stiglitz notes, if oil companies do these things in the United States, one can imagine that the abuses are much worse in countries where institutions are weaker. Stiglitz argues that there are no easy answers to the resource curse. He stresses, however, the importance of transparency in the agreements between mineral companies and governments. He also argues that the country itself should remain the ultimate owner of the resource and that there should be a fair division of the earnings from the resources. Companies should be compensated for the risks they take, but when the price of the mineral increases, the increased earnings should go primarily to the country and not the company.

Oil is only one of the minerals whose extraction is causing great suffering. Let me conclude this brief survey of ill-gotten minerals by discussing rare earth metals. They are less well known than oil or coal, but they are omnipresent in our lives. They too show how the lives of even middle-class people are built upon the suffering of the poor in ways that the middle class may not have noticed. Absent rare earth metals, there would be no mobile phones, no computers, no flat-screen monitors or flat-screen TVs. Absent rare earth metals, the virtuous would not be driving hybrid cars and/or getting "green" energy from modern windmills. Absent rare earth metals, there would be no internet. The great innovation in the public sphere of today—the internet—is built upon the exploitation of many, largely unseen.

Today 95 percent of all rare earth metals are mined in China. Almost half of the world's supply comes from one mine near Baotou. Baotou is the largest city in the Inner Mongolian Autonomous Region. It is very hard to mine these minerals and then refine them in an ecologically sensitive way. Next to the plants that refine these minerals is a four-square-kilometer reservoir where sludge from the plants is stored. The sludge is slightly radioactive and full of toxic chemicals. [12] As a *New York Times* article points out, China, or more precisely the people of Baotou, are doing the world's dirty work. Rare minerals are not really rare. They are found the world over. According to some estimates only 35 percent of the world's supply of these metals is found in China. At one time, there were rare earth metal mines in many parts of the world. Almost all other countries have shut down their mines and allowed the Chinese—or more specifically the people of Baotou—to bear the environmental costs of extracting them. The reservoir in Baotou is only seven miles from the watershed that supplies the Yellow River, and the Yellow River supplies much of northern China with its drinking water. The bottom of the reservoir is not properly lined so the contamination is slowly spreading toward the Yellow River watershed, threatening the drinking water supply upon which most of northern China depends. In addition, there are many illegal unregulated rare earth metal mines in southern China that are doing serious environmental damage. [13] The virtual world is literally built on the environmental degradation of Baotou and many other parts of China.

China and India are growing wealthy and they are hunting for natural resources. They seem prepared—just like the United States—to compromise with dictators to procure the mineral goods. President Obiang's (of Equatorial Guinea) access to the United States stands as a telling witness of the power of minerals to corrupt the U.S. political process, not to mention its banking system. How can we join with others—for example, Chinese activists, to ensure that China's hunger for Sudan's oil wealth does not lead them to sanction President Omar al-Bashir's repression in Sudan? Or how do we join with Indian activists to make sure that India's desire for mineral wealth does not prop up oppressive regimes in other countries? The fact that others are ready to buy these ill-gotten minerals if we don't makes things more complicated, but I doubt this absolves us of all moral responsibility. Just because many people participated in the Holocaust, we do not excuse anyone. We do make a distinction between those who enthusiastically participated and those who were forced to participate. Of course today in the United States I am not living in a totalitarian regime. No one is forcing me to drive in the same way that some were forced to participate in the Holocaust. On the other hand, given the lack of public transportation, I would not have my job if I did not drive my car and I could not do my job without my computer. Given my relative freedom what can I do to reduce my contributions to the problem of ill-gotten mineral wealth? My point is not to make us feel guilty, but to make us think about what we might do to push the world in a more just direction. I am not suggesting that this is only the case where we should take individual actions. Reforming the way the world extracts minerals will take social change as well, but individual acts and broad social movements for social change can go hand in hand.

The citizens of Baotou are not the only ones endangered because of rare earth metals. All of us who own cell phones own coltan, another rare earth metal. The Congo is rich in coltan. Coltan is in short supply and many of the militias that are behind the rape epidemics in the Congo are supporting themselves through the sale of this metal. In the Congo, as in most places where mineral wealth is found, this wealth is empowering a few who are then ruthlessly exploiting others. The world came together to put a stop to the blood diamonds, but the UN has reported, as recently as the summer of 2010, that militias were raping women and boys in the region where coltan is mined. In response to these reports, the Dodd-Frank Wall Street Reform Act contained a provision that requires publicly traded companies to explain what measures they are taking to ensure that the money that procures the minerals used in their supply chains is not enriching the warlords of the Congo. Some are now claiming that this provision is having the unintended effect of simply shutting down the mining industry in eastern Congo and harming the very people it was intended to help. David Aronson claims that local miners, high level traders, mining companies and civil society leaders are unanimous in condemning the Dodd-Frank bill.[14] Poignantly, Aronson ends the article by quoting Eric Kajemba, who Aronson says asked him ("more in confusion than in anger"), "If the advocacy groups aren't speaking for the people of eastern Congo, whom are they speaking for?" I have no doubt that the Dodd-Frank bill was well-intentioned, and it is certainly impossible to say on the basis of one reporter's claims that the bill is having unintended consequences. There is no doubt that the people of eastern Congo are suffering. The challenge is to figure out how to help. Certainly it is absolutely essential for those who are affected to be partners in the search for a solution.

Minerals almost never bring wealth to those who inhabit the lands where they are found. The more we learn about rare earth metal and oil extraction, the more we will be able to understand the exploitation that makes our lifestyles possible. The lives of the middle class are made possible by the exploitation of people all over the world. What has famously been said about oil can be applied to mineral wealth in general and rare earth metals in particular: They "anesthetize thought, blur vision and corrupt."[15] As Sen argues, we can recognize obvious injustice, even if we do not have a perfectly formed theory of justice. As we learn more about the exploitation that makes our lives possible, there is little doubt that many who live on top of mineral wealth are not receiving justice and that they are suffering so that we might live our middle-class lives.

Sen is right that the ethical problem is not hard to see, but the solutions are often not easy to find. And even if we think we understand what should be done it is often hard to know how any one individual can bring about the needed change. If I alone stopped using fossil fuels tomorrow nothing would change. Not being able to drive my gas-powered car to work, I would lose my job, and the people of the Niger Delta, the Oriente region, and Angola would still be poor. Clearly, we need to work with others to change the way the oil is extracted, we need to reduce our carbon footprint even as we encourage others to reduce their carbon footprint, and we need to work against the corruption that seems to follow the oil industry wherever it goes (with the possible exception of Norway). Singer's solution to world poverty seems easy. It is particularly easy for professors since Singer asks very little from those making less than $100,000 a year. Given that it costs so little, it is worth giving something to charity as we work to make deeper systemic changes. But the people of the Niger Delta and the Oriente, Angola, Equatorial Guinea, and Baotou, to name just a few of the places that have been devastated by the extraction of minerals, do not need our charity. They need our help to fight against the power of oil companies and their own corrupt politicians and business leaders.

The world is increasingly, as Sen notes, not only joined by economic concerns, but also by our shared concerns about injustice and the threat of terrorism.[16] Sen admits that the notions of justice behind these concerns may be "vaguely shared," but they are not totally disparate. As the recent protests in the Middle East so dramatically illustrate, appeals for justice and democracy resonate deeply in many different parts of the globe. Many in the world are united not only by our frustrations about the lack of progress on issues of social justice, but also by our hopes for a more just world. The well-being of the vast majority of first world and third world peoples will rely on building principled coalitions across the first world/third world divide. The oil spill in the Gulf of Mexico illustrates how the failure to address injustice in a seemingly distant part of the world may contribute to "spill over" problems in our own backyard. Working together across national boundaries we can form principled coalitions that pressure oil companies to be more ethical. Shell clearly does things in the Niger Delta that they would not dream of doing in other countries where they are active. If its corporate culture has allowed for the devastation of the Niger Delta we shouldn't be surprised if Shell is not always ethical in its dealings in the first world. In short, we in the first world would be wise to listen to the people of the Niger Delta not only so that we might aid them, but also because it will end up benefitting us. It is important for those of us in the first world to publicize the exploitation in the Third World and work to change its corporate practices. And once we have heard from the Niger Delta, we might turn our eyes to the development of the Athabasca oil sands of Canada—where Shell is active—and with activists there seek to limit the damage that is done. I have not gone into it, but there is certainly evidence that coal has brought great suffering and little wealth to the vast majority of the people of West Virginia. In some ways it is easier to see the corruption brought by minerals in Africa, but it is naïve to think that mineral wealth is not affecting politics in the first world as well.[17]

I don't see much point in arguing about whether or not we have obligations to the distant needy when so many of the distant needy are in one way or another suffering at the hands of those who are supplying me with the raw materials in the things I use every day. Today, the distant needy are really not so distant and those who live in relative physical proximity are often not acting very neighborly. Who is our sister? The women from the Congo who suffered so that I might make a cell phone call or the Goldman Sachs banker whose risky practices brought the world economy to the brink of collapse? Are the oil company executives my brothers? On the one hand, they are out scouring the world so that I might drive my car. But if we allow unethical business practices to ravage the poor, we should not be surprised if these same businesses end up exploiting the middle class when it serves their interests. The well-being of the industrialized world and the nonindustrialized world will rely on building principled coalitions between distant peoples. Given how much the people of the Niger Delta, Ecuador, Angola, Equatorial Guinea, and almost every other place where oil is being extracted have sacrificed to allow me to drive my car, they are much more my brothers—admittedly a brother who has been suffering abuse so that I might live my middle-class life—than the bankers who recklessly exploited lax financial regulations. Many of the global poor have insights about justice that I and the investment bankers, and those involved in mineral extraction, really should hear. If we listen to the global poor we just might rethink our lives a bit, and work harder to curb our use of minerals and change the economic systems and corporate practices that exploit the world's poor. One learns a great deal by watching how the powerful act when they think no one is watching. Together we might tame the beasts, for example, the large multinational corporations and corrupt governments whose exploitation make our lives possible, not to mention our own beastly capacious energy-intensive lifestyles.

The internet offers more than porn, spam, shopping, and movies. It allows us to keep track of the civilian body count in Iraq (Iraqbodycount.org) and perhaps that will lead us to fight harder and more effectively next time to stop an unjustified war. It also offers us the chance to connect with others who are laboring on our behalf. The internet allows us to trace how the lifestyles of the middle class the world over are interconnected with the suffering of the poor. Rare earth metals make the internet possible, and the internet can in turn make visible the suffering of people all over the world, so it seems very apt that we should use the public space that the internet pro vides to connect with others and fight so that the Niger Delta and the Oriente is cleaned the Nigerians and the people of Equatorial Guinea receive the benefits from the minerals which have until now only brought suffering to the vast majority. And in reining in these abuses of the poor, we will be making the world a safer place for ourselves.

Thomas Pogge is more specific in his prescriptions about how to address the mineral curse. He argues that the sale of a nation's resources should not be considered legitimate unless the sale is in accord with what he calls "broadly democratic authorization." To allow oppressive regimes to sell resources is to invite predators to take power. Pogge suggests that resource-rich states should insert a provision in their constitution that would provide for the selection of "trusted experts" who would judge whether or not the sale of resources was truly authorized by the people. If these experts judged that a regime was not acting on behalf of the will of the people, then together with the United Nations, the sales would be viewed as unauthorized and Pogge believes this would cause a nation to think twice about purchasing them. I admire Pogge for admitting that this plan might not work. Nonetheless, he argues for it on the basis that it would "clarify the moral situation." Pogge hopes that such mechanisms might also increase awareness in wealthy nations of how our lifestyles are supporting corrupt regimes such as the one in Equatorial Guinea.[18]

Joshua Cohen criticizes Pogge for having "overly ambitious" hopes about the efficacy of making changes in international rules of commerce. Cohen argues that we cannot know exactly how changes in international rules will affect countries internally. Cohen questions whether Pogge's suggested changes to international rules of ownership would really lead to the reduction in poverty that Pogge thinks they would.[19] The idea behind the changes Pogge suggests is that they would make it harder for despots to borrow money, squander it and then leave the debt for future generations. It is hard to argue with Cohen's conclusion that calls for us to be open-minded, empirical, and experimental in order to learn about what changes in domestic and international institutions might best alleviate poverty. Sen also criticizes Pogge for having too much faith in his ability to design a transcendentally just set of institutions for the entire world.[20]

I agree with Pogge that institutions are important, but I am less certain that, as a philosopher, I am in a position to recommend an institution, particularly an institution to a country in the global south. As we will see shortly, the International Monetary Fund (IMF), to name just one institution, has made many recommendations to the global south that have turned out badly. Philosophers can raise awareness of injustice. As citizens and consumers, all of us can press our governments to take steps to reduce the exploitation. For example, we can lobby to require oil companies to publish how much they are paying to governments for their oil and to forbid these companies from paying bribes. These two steps have, according to some, reduced the corruption in the extraction of minerals. Again, the fact that oil companies such as Chevron have run "public service announcements" on public television in the United States shows that they are wary of public opinion. Pogge and I do agree that the people in developed countries need to pay more attention to how their use of minerals is adversely affecting many nations. I would add that it is also affecting many people in West Virginia, on the Gulf of Mexico coast of the United States, and in other places in the United States. All of us who are using mineral resources have a moral obligation to join with the people who are suffering to publicize their plight and *with those who are being harmed* to lobby to change corporate behavior. Publicizing the suffering that mineral wealth has wrought can help the efforts to contain these multinational behemoths in the first world and third world. Given the worries that corporations have about their brands, activists may have an easier time changing corporate practices than governmental policies. [21]

A STRUCTURAL ADJUSTMENT FOR THE INTERNATIONAL MONETARY FUND

One of the most forceful advocates for the reforming of international economic relations has been Joseph Stiglitz. [22] Stiglitz won the Nobel Prize in economics, was a member of President Bill Clinton's Council of Economic Advisers and, from 1997–2000, was chief economist and senior vice president for the World Bank. He argues very forcefully that the International Monetary Fund has repeatedly given bad economic advice to third world countries and imposed draconian measures that have not only failed to revive third world economies, but have plunged millions of people into poverty. [23]

Originally set up to maintain global economic stability and to prevent another Great Depression, the IMF is an international organization, but the United States is the only country that has a veto power over its decisions. Unlike the IMF, the chief mission of the World Bank is to reduce global poverty. Stiglitz's critiques are the dissent of someone who has had access to decision-making processes at a very high level. His books reveal some of the disagreements about policy that were going on in the United States' government as well as the disagreements between the World Bank and the IMF. One of his goals is to foster more open discussion of IMF and World Bank policies.

Stiglitz argues that the IMF managed the East Asian crisis that began in 1997 and the transition of the Russian economy particularly badly. In fairness to the IMF, Stiglitz notes that in the case of Russia the IMF was doing something that had never been done before, namely, trying to move an economy from socialism to capitalism in a short time. Nevertheless, it is undeniable that the lives of ordinary people in Asia and in Russia were devastated, in part, as a result of the decisions imposed by the IMF, and it is doubtful that many of the measures the IMF proposed were either necessary or even helpful to the economies of these countries. Many people in the global north do not know much about the IMF and World Bank, but many of the citizens of the third world know these organizations well. Their lives are often directly impacted by the programs the IMF imposes. For many of the people of the global south the IMF is a household word and it has been so for a long time. In response to the IMF proscriptions in 1976 there were riots in Egypt where more than seven hundred people died. In the 1990s protestors carried signs in Jakarta that read "Michel Camdessus [then managing director of the IMF] go home!" Small wonder that they did so, when the IMF insisted that Indonesia abolish subsidies for food and kerosene—the fuel that the poor use to cook their food. The IMF-ordered curbs in government food subsidies directly affect millions of the most vulnerable people.

Stiglitz claims that the IMF was correct when it sought to curb the spending of several South American countries during the 1980s. These countries were pursuing loose monetary policies. Their large deficits produced inflation and curbing government expenditures was necessary. But the IMF fundamentally misdiagnosed the problem in East Asia that began when the Thai baht collapsed on July 2, 1997. These countries were not engaged in deficit spending. Their economies were fundamentally sound. One of the IMF's key mistakes, Stiglitz argues, was its insistence that the East Asian economies liberalize their currency controls. This liberalization allowed for currency speculation. Only Malaysia bucked the IMF during this crisis and imposed controls to limit the flow of speculative capital. As a result, its crisis was shorter and less profound than that of any of the other countries.[24] In response to the crisis, the IMF arranged for $95 billion to be loaned to East Asian countries to maintain, at least for a time, their exchange rates. This in turn allowed the country to repay loans to Western banks. But in the long run the countries were not able to maintain their currencies, and when the currencies collapsed the loans from the IMF became much more expensive to repay. In other words, the loans did very little for the countries themselves; they mainly benefited Western economies and, in particular, Western banks. Least we think that the world has learned from Stiglitz's analysis, we need only to note that in subsequent trade deals the United States insisted on strong prohibitions on Chile and Morocco that would prevent them from imposing the kinds of monetary controls that would be needed if there were to be a run on their currencies. Such a policy might help Western financial institutions in the short run, but it flies in the face of the lessons learned from the East Asian crisis. This IMF policy directly benefits many first world pension funds serving academics like myself that, according to the International Labor Organization, are heavily invested in the stock markets of middle-income countries.[25]

In addition to privileging first world investors, the IMF has a history of bad decisions. In response to the East Asian crisis, the IMF forced East Asian countries to curtail government spending. The countries of East Asia invested in education and industry in order to raise the standard of living for their people. Furthermore, these countries *were not* running structural deficits at the time the crisis hit. As a condition of receiving their desperately needed loans, the IMF demanded that these countries raise their interest rates, cut back government spending and increase taxes. In cutting back money in areas such as education, the IMF was acting to undermine one of the most important engines of economic growth. At the very time when the East Asian economies were experiencing a precipitous fall in demand, the IMF proscribed decreasing government expenditures, increasing taxes, and increasing interest rates. In other words, in a time of economic crisis we demanded that the East Asian countries do things that no U.S. government has done in the face of economic crisis since Herbert Hoover. The United States is loath to raise taxes, increase interest rates, and decrease government spending in relatively good economic times. To repeat the point, unlike the United States, at the time of the East Asian crisis the governments were not running structural deficits. As a result of the crisis, and the IMF imposed conditions, unemployment went up fourfold in Korea and threefold in Thailand.[26] In South Korea almost a quarter of the population fell into poverty.[27] The countries that followed the IMF policies most closely, Thailand and Indonesia, had much slower recoveries than countries such as South Korea and Malaysia that charted a more independent path. In short, the IMF imposed conditions on these countries that brought enormous amounts of suffering to large numbers of people. When the United States or the IMF imposes conditions that favor first world banks and first world pension funds to the detriment of third world citizens we are actively involved in bringing poverty to the third world so that we, actually our financial institutions, might prosper.

Stiglitz does not suggest that the IMF deliberately gave bad economic advice nor that it deliberately ran the economies of East Asia into the ground in order to bail out Western banks, but clearly the IMF made mistakes and the policies did aid Western banks to the detriment of these countries. The IMF directed the East Asian countries to protect their currencies and lent them money to do this. The currencies were propped up for a short time and this allowed many Western financial institutions to recoup a portion of their loans. Once the currencies fell, however, the countries were left with huge loans that they could no longer repay. Furthermore, the policy of forcing these countries to raise interest rates, cut government expenditures and increase taxes in the failed effort to protect exchange rates led to the collapse of many businesses and, as Stiglitz notes, it is much easier to ruin a company than to build it up. The IMF justifies many of its proscriptions under the rubric of painful medicine. There is little evidence that the medicine produced much in the way of benefits.

The IMF preaches free market solutions, but it does not want any competition. Japan offered $100 billion to start an Asian Monetary Fund in 1997. The money would have been used to stimulate the markets, but the IMF opposed the creation of the fund. Eventually the IMF relented and took $30 billion from Japan for itself, but insisted that the money not be used for stimulus, but rather to help bail out foreign banks.[28] Until recent events in Greece and Spain, no Western nation, since the Great Depression, has faced an economic downturn with the measures proscribed. Western nations have always turned to stimulus to confront recessions, but the IMF not only refused to promote stimulus for the East Asian economies, it also actively blocked Japan's effort to stimulate demand in East Asia. Even the IMF now admits that it made mistakes in the East Asian crisis and it has apologized for the austerity it imposed. These days the IMF is even encouraging Western nations to do more stimulus. One of the things holding back the world economy today is the large amount of reserves that many third world countries feel they must hold so that they never again will need to go to the IMF for loans. If these nations would spend some of those reserves wisely they could address the poverty in their nations. That these nations continue to hold large reserves is a testament to how deeply scarred they are from the austerity measures imposed during the 1990s. The notion of accountability is on a remarkable number lips these days. It is certainly a word omnipresent in the "welfare reform" debates that took place in the United States in the 1990s. To the extent that the U.S. government actively supported the misguided policies of the IMF, the United States clearly has a responsibility to help fix what it helped to break. We allowed or even encouraged the IMF to act in support of Western financial institutions at tremendous cost to the citizens of the countries involved. I have not benefited as much as the wealthy shareholders of these banks or the officers of these banks, but I did benefit insofar as these measures help to protect my investment for retirement. In a world that is increasingly interconnected it is in our interest to promote the economic well-being of others. Indonesia, a country particularly hard-hit by the East Asian crisis, is also a country where a fundamentalist Islamic terrorist organization is at work. If capitalism does not own up to its failures and respond to the needs and aspirations of the masses, other ideologies will.

The failures of the IMF should serve as a lesson to all who would *impose* international schemes—be they schemes of trade or systems of justice. Much of the criticism of the IMF is that it was too heavy-handed. With too little understanding of the countries where they were intervening and blinded by ideological prejudice about free markets, the IMF imposed ill-advised policies on countries. Philosophers are sometimes accused of similar failings.

Plato infamously went to Sicily to help Dionysius II structure the ideal state and ended up under house arrest. Theory often withers under the pressure of the real world. No one has all the answers. Ethical responses and social policies aimed at fixing the problems posed by our complex world must be constructed through careful deliberation, with much humility and in dialogue with all the affected parties. Sen is right that injustice is easy to see. As I have already noted, the problem is that it is often much harder to understand how to bring about justice. It is foolish to think that it is only the IMF that makes mistakes when trying to help.

AGRICULTURAL SUBSIDIES AND IMPORT RESTRICTIONS

If we want to reduce poverty in the world, we need to implement policies that will help where help is most needed. Given that the majority of people in the global South are employed in agriculture we must find ways to help these people climb out of poverty. Agricultural subsidies and limitations on the import of crops are one of the most prominent examples of first world policies that often adversely affect poor third world citizens. These policies also do not help most citizens of wealthy countries because they siphon off much-needed government money to support wealthy agricultural corporations or at times they take money directly from the pockets of first world consumers by forcing them to pay higher prices. Most poor farmers are net sellers of food or sellers of their agricultural labor, so a decrease in export subsidies on Northern agricultural products or allowing more Southern goods into wealthy Northern nations would put money into the pockets of Southern agricultural workers.[29] Without selling some of the things they grow, these farmers cannot get money for education and health care that will allow them and their families to climb out of poverty. It is hard to see how we can help these farmers without changing the subsidies and import controls that depress their earnings.

For example, farmers in Uganda have used the money they earned from growing and selling coffee to buy pigs and goats. They are fortunate that coffee is not grown with subsidies in Europe or the United States. They have also used the money that coffee brought in to learn how to sell vegetables for export.[30] When the farmers become wealthier they have more money to spend in the local community, to hire farm laborers and construction workers, and to buy things in their local markets. As long as the United States continues to subsidize its cotton growers, how could West African cotton farmers, to take one example, benefit from aid that would help them improve their crops? If we only gave these farmers aid to help them increase their crop yields or crop quality, they would still have to compete against the more heavily subsidized U.S. crops. There are an estimated 10 million farmers in West Africa who can grow cotton cheaper than the highly mechanized and highly subsidized farmers of West Texas. They may also grow it in a way that produces fewer greenhouse gases. Almost all countries subsidize, to some extent, agricultural products, but the subsidies that the United States pays its wealthy farmers are more than most countries. According to one estimate, the elimination of U.S. cotton subsidies would cause the world price for cotton to rise and thereby provide enough extra income to feed more than a million children in cotton-growing families in Benin, Burkina Faso, Chad and Mali.[31] Left in place the subsidies make it difficult for the African farmer to compete and lower the value of his or her cotton.[32]

In some cases elimination of export subsidies and production subsidies could lead to an increase in prices in developing countries and this could disadvantage the working poor in urban areas. Overall, Stiglitz and Charlton suggest that the elimination of production subsidies and export subsidies would probably advantage agricultural exporting nations such as Brazil and Australia. It could hurt some urban poor in some developing nations while helping many in the agricultural sectors in the South. They suggest that every country is different and care must be taken to consider the individual circumstances of each country, but on the whole the benefits that accompany liberalizing agricultural trade outweigh the disadvantages. Moreover, steps can be taken to mitigate the effect that these reforms have on, for example, the urban poor.

Without the subsidies and import controls, cotton and sugar, in particular, could be grown more cheaply in many poor third world nations. While it is true that the price of cotton and sugar might rise, this would put more money into the hands of the agricultural sectors of cotton- and sugar-producing countries. Increases in cotton and sugar prices would also not affect the urban poor as much as increases in the price of basic foodstuffs. In addition, the price of cotton is such a small part of the cost of the finished garment that an increase in the cost of cotton does not have that much of an effect on the cost of the garment. But the rural poor are not the only ones who would benefit. For example, of the $130 billion the United States gave in agricultural subsidies between 1996 and 2005, the vast majority went to five crops: corn, wheat, soybeans, cotton, and rice. Two-thirds of American farmers get no subsidies at all.[33] Sugar is not subsidized, but the American sugar industry benefits from restrictions on the importation of sugar. In order to show how these import restrictions harm people in both the third and the first world, let us look more closely at the case of sugar.

Import controls on sugar have resulted, at times (depending upon the markets), in consumers in the United States paying three times the world price for sugar. These controls directly benefit only a small number of politically connected individuals and a relatively small number of workers. It is estimated that there are only sixty-one thousand jobs in the United States directly tied to growing sugar. The limits on importing sugar are, however, costing jobs in other sectors such as the production of candy. Several U.S. candy manufacturers have moved production to Canada and Mexico. *New York Times* articles from 2005 and 2013 both quoted executives of candy companies that moved who claimed that the candy factory was not moved because of labor costs. Labor constitutes only 3 to 6 percent of the cost of candy, while sugar can represent 30 to 70 percent of the candy's cost.[34] In other words, these import limitations and subsidies are not even good for the U.S. economy. They cost more jobs than they protect. The growing of sugar is also environmentally damaging to the Everglades. The sugar farms of South Florida are diverting enormous amounts of water that could be used to restore this unique and very beautiful ecosystem.

There is a similar problem with catfish and shrimp, which are cheaper to raise in places like Vietnam and China. In response, the U.S. government has placed large import duties on them. Addressing the systems that undergird global poverty may mean, in some cases, no sacrifice at all for many of us. Consumers in the United States end up paying higher prices to protect politically well-connected companies. Good public policy on trade would help rural populations in the developing world and U.S. consumers as well as many Northern businesses —for example, candy makers and restaurants that buy shrimp—and disadvantage relatively few. Some U.S. workers would be affected, but we would be better off using the money spent on subsidies on the retraining of workers rather than supporting inefficient industries.

In making his case that the proper ethical response to global inequalities is to give money to charities, Singer noted that even George Bush called the 2008 farm bill wasted and bloated and vetoed it, but the United States Congress easily overcame his veto. This suggests to Singer that our efforts to make systemic changes in government policy in this area are doomed to failure.[35] Given the downturn in the U.S. economy in 2008 and the desire of many to rein in deficits, U.S.agricultural subsidies seemed more vulnerable now than they were in 2008. Unfortunately, the most recent farm bill, passed in 2014, seems to have left many of the subsidies in place. Ironically, it did reduce the amount of money going to subsidize food for the poor in the United States.

Change to these wasteful policies may come as a result of other players outside the United States. In response to a complaint brought by Brazil, the U.S. subsidies on cotton have been ruled illegal by the World Trade Organization. As a result, Brazil was granted the right to impose $800 million worth of import duties on products from the United States. To ward off that, the United States has agreed to pay $147.3 million a year to set up a technical assistance fund as well as (among other things) modify a loan program that foreign buyers use to purchase U.S. agricultural products.[36] It seems that one of the main motivations for settling the dispute was Brazil's receiving permission from the WTO to break U.S. patent laws and stop charging its farmers fees for seeds developed by U.S. agricultural companies. Brazil's threat to break patents on U.S. seeds cleverly targeted a sector of the United States' economy that is deeply involved in agricultural policy. A newly emergent power, Brazil, is using the WTO to fight for the rights of its citizens. To the extent that Brazil succeeds in curtailing U.S. cotton subsidies, it is also fighting for the interests of the vast majority of U.S. citizens. Unfortunately, in this case, the subsidies were not curbed—Brazil was given money to compensate for its losses and that allowed the subsidies to remain in place.

Some have argued that Brazil's actions are deeply hypocritical given its own subsidies to its cotton growers. One source estimates that Brazil provides an even greater subsidy to its cotton farmers than the United States does.[37] I will leave it to others to argue about who gives the greater subsidy, but even if Brazil does give a greater subsidy that still does not mean that the United States should be subsidizing its cotton growers. There may well be an argument for subsidies to preserve food production capability, but even though I wear almost exclusively cotton clothing, I would argue it is not in the United States' vital interest to preserve the capability for large-scale cotton farming. Of course one should be concerned about the dislocation that would be caused in the United States by the ending of these subsidies, but we could protect the most vulnerable by capping the subsidies at first and then gradually eliminating them. What is truly indefensible is the giving of subsidies to large agribusinesses when there are many more important unmet needs. Why should the United States be giving subsidies to wealthy cotton farmers when, for example, many children in the United States are attending substandard schools?

Corruption and crony capitalism are clearly not just third world problems. The truly modest proposal to limit agricultural subsidies to $250,000 per farmer was fought vigorously by the powerful and the limit was never imposed. The United States preaches free trade, but does not practice what it preaches. It has been widely recognized that previous trade negotiations have yielded little benefit to developing nations and this round, commonly referred to as the Doha Round, was supposed to remedy that problem.[38] At one point the effort to come to an agreement failed largely because the United States and India could not agree. India wanted the right to protect its farmers (75 percent of its population, many of whom are poor) if foreign food started flooding its market. India may have learned a lesson from NAFTA, which made poor Mexican farmers compete with subsidized U.S. farm products. At the same time, the United States took action to keep cheaper Mexican tomatoes out of the United States.[39] There is great poverty in the rural areas of Mexico. Four-fifths of the rural population of Mexico lives in poverty and more than half of these live in extreme poverty, and NAFTA has exacerbated it.[40] Some have argued that oil money has not hurt Mexico, but Mexico invested little money in education and technology for many years. For example, China invests almost twice as much of its GNP in these areas as Mexico does. Mexico also does not invest as much in these areas as Brazil does.[41] It is important to remember that NAFTA was negotiated at a time when Mexico was largely under one-party rule. NAFTA has simply not attended to the interests of Mexico's poor rural population, and the fact that the government gets significant revenues from the oil industry means that its public policies do not have to attend to the needs of its people as closely. If most of its revenues were coming from tax revenues, the taxpayers would be much more likely to demand that the government policies reflect their interests.

The Indian government's concern for the rural farmers was not purely altruistic. The elections of 2004 in India were interpreted by many as the protest of rural Indians who had not shared in the country's economic boom. In the 2004 national elections the Hindu Fundamentalist Party or BJP ran on the slogan "India Shining," but the rural poor who had not shared in the economic upswing voted the BJP out of office. Even today, nearly 65 percent of all Indians live in rural areas.[42] In response, the Congress government paid more attention to the needs of the rural population. It, for example, instituted an employment scheme whereby rural workers were guaranteed three months of labor every year. Congress won reelection by wide margins, but then was soundly trounced in 2014. The BJP regained power on the promises of economic development rather than religious appeals. It remains to be seen if the BJP's promises (for example, electricity and sanitation for all) will be fulfilled. Its record on human development in Gujarat was not good.

In short, IMF policies and agricultural policies of wealthy nations really matter to the poor of the third world.[43] All too often these policies have worked against the poor. In many cases they have benefitted only a few well-connected elites. If one looks to where poverty reduction has been most successful, it has happened where public policies have been implemented that enabled the poor to climb out of poverty. India and Brazil are democracies that have acted to protect the interests of some of their most vulnerable citizens. I do not doubt Singer's claim that agricultural subsidies and import restrictions will be hard to rein in, but given how important the reduction of rural poverty is in the fight against global poverty, it is incumbent upon us to try, and it is not just first world activists who are in this fight. Those who find these subsidies unjust have powerful allies such as the governments of Brazil and India.

INTERNATIONAL LABOR STANDARDS

I take it as a first principle that workers should not be exploited. By exploited I mean, among other things, that workers should earn a living wage. Exactly what constitutes a living wage will vary greatly from place to place, but it should be enough to supply the worker and his or her family with food, lodging, health care, and leisure time. The International Labor Organization (ILO) was established in 1919 by the Treaty of Versailles, as a part of the League of Nations, and it is the only major creation of that treaty that survives today. It became the first specialized agency of the United Nations in 1946. From its inception it has been composed of representatives of workers, employers and governments. Its goal is to promote social justice through the promotion of human and labor rights.[44] One hundred and seventy-seven countries are members of the ILO. It has formulated two core conventions to articulate the rights of workers: The Freedom of Association and Protection of the Right to Organize Convention (1948) and The Right to Organize and Collective Bargaining Convention (1949). The first convention has been ratified by 142 member states. The second convention has been ratified by 149 member states. Unfortunately, almost half of the workers of the world live in nations that have not ratified the two conventions; Brazil, China, India, Mexico, and the United States are among the largest nations that have not signed the conventions. In 1998, the ILO issued the Declaration of Fundamental Rights at Work. The declaration contains four "core labor standards": freedom of association and the right to collective bargaining, abolition of compulsory labor, the abolition of child labor and freedom from discrimination. Maria C. Mattioli and V.K. Sapovadia note that the World Bank offers two justifications for Core Labor Standards.[45] The standards help to reduce poverty and they contribute to social and economic development. For example, to the extent that children labor excessively, their education is neglected. An educated workforce is an important part of economic development. Therefore, the elimination of child labor can aid development. Similarly, a culture of negotiation and the raising of the standard of living contribute to stability in countries in the south and hence encourage investment. Mattioli and Sapovadia also argue that the Core Labor Standards help to ensure that companies will be less likely to suffer bad publicity and consumer boycotts. Instead of seeing the call for labor standards as a protectionist measure, Mattioli and Sapovadia see the standards as a boon to countries of both the north and the south. Morality is not the only reason to protect workers' rights. Development, stability and the protection of worker's rights go hand in hand.

Those of us who live in countries that are not party to these agreements should lobby our governments to sign them and then encourage other nations that have not yet done so to do the same. It is hard to tell others to do what we have not done ourselves, but I am under no illusions that the U.S. government will sign these conventions anytime soon, but there are things we can do as individuals. Given how hard it is to prod our governments to act, we should act as individuals. Through carefully selecting the products we buy, we can promote workers' rights. Paul Krugman, in the famous article "In Praise of Cheap Labor: Bad jobs are better than no jobs at all"[46] claims that those, like myself, who would argue for international labor standards risk harming the very people they are trying to help. First world countries have formidable advantages and raising the labor costs in third world countries may erode their competitive advantage. Forcing the factories to pay better wages may encourage jobs to leave these countries and leave people worse off, hence the claim that bad jobs are better than no jobs at all. It has been more than fifteen years since Krugman wrote this article and I doubt he would still say that third world countries are at risk of losing these jobs to first world countries. Today, the danger seems to be that third world countries may lose their jobs to other third world countries. Very few jobs seem to be flowing back to the first world from the third world, but Krugman's point is well-taken. How are we to insure that crusading for workers' rights will not end up costing workers their livelihoods? History is full of well-intentioned crusades gone wrong.

Krugman writes that the demands for international labor standards come out of a self-righteous feeling that we in the first world do not want people working at slave wages for our benefit. The demand that workers receive living wages may mean that they receive no wages at all. Some have questioned whether one should prohibit the use of child labor. It has been widely reported that the passage of the Harkin Bill in the United States in 1993, a bill that prohibited the importation of goods made with child labor, resulted in fifty thousand children losing their factory jobs in Bangladesh in 1994. Many of these children turned to jobs as stone crushers, street hustlers, or prostitutes and made less money and endured even worse working conditions than they had in sweatshops. Many poor families do realize the importance of educating their children. A study done in Vietnam showed that as soon as parents could afford to cover their family's basic needs they would usually take their children out of the workforce and send them to school, even if this meant a reduction in family income.[47] For the very poor, sending their children to work in a sweatshop may be the only way to make enough money to survive. Taking a page from Aristotle, one could argue that the Harkin Bill, however well-intentioned, failed the test of prudence, but there are good reasons to believe that the promotion of workers' rights does not always harm the worker.[48]

An international labor rights group has plans to sue the United States Customs service for allowing "African coca picked by indentured child labor to be imported into this country" (the United States). Plantation owners buy children from neighboring countries to pick the coca beans. This practice of using indentured child labor was documented in a 1998 report by UNICEF's Ivory Coast office. The U.S. State Department's 2002 report on human rights states that "some forced child labor and trafficking in children and women . . . persists."[49] A targeted suit aimed at particularly egregious situations, like the situation in the Ivory Coast, is most likely better than a sweeping solution that is bound to have adverse unintended consequences. Krugman is right to warn that self-righteousness is a danger lurking in every attempt at moral philosophy. And I have already freely admitted that one must also always be on guard against the danger that one's moral theorizing may end up making things worse. As Stiglitz and Charlton—or for that matter Aristotle—argue, we must be attuned to the particular situation.

The Multi-Fiber agreement expired on January 1, 2005. This agreement was first signed in 1974 and then modified under the auspices of the Uruguay Round Agreement on Textiles and Clothing (ATC) which came into effect on January 1, 1995. With the agreement's expiration on January 1, 2005, the limits on importation of garments from China expired as well, and this has led to many jobs being shifted to China where wages are low and independent unions are banned. China abounds in hi-tech machinery and its infrastructure is modern. China has such a large workforce that many believe that it alone is capable of clothing the world.

As an example of the very thing he warns against, Krugman could cite the plight of a woman described in an article from July 2004 in *The Independent*.[50] The article tells of a twenty-seven-year-old woman named Warmi who worked fourteen-hour days sewing backpacks for Adidas and JanSport in Indonesia. She earned about $90 dollars a month, which was enough to support her three children and elderly parents. The plant is about to close and the production will be shifted to China. What makes Warmi's story particularly painful is that the company for which she worked, a Korean firm named Dae Joo, was investigated by Worker's Rights Consortium, an organization based in Washington, D.C. that investigates goods carrying the logo of U.S. universities. The investigation revealed that the Dae Joo plant was not even complying with Indonesian laws. Dae Joo agreed to make major changes and the factory became a model workplace. Among other changes, health care was extended to the employees and their families. The plant's production was then moved to the Dae Joo plant in Qingdao, China.

Even in China there are jobs being lost as the industry grows more efficient. From 1995–2002 the Chinese textile industry lost more than 1.8 million jobs, while the United States lost 202,000 textile jobs. During this time, China's labor productivity rose by more than 300 percent. In other words, productivity gains are leading to job losses in China.[51] China is not going to clothe the world. Recently China has actually been losing jobs to countries where wages are even lower. Despite both the increased efficiency and the emergence of lower-wage producers, the Pearl River Delta and the Yangtze

River Delta (the regions in China most devoted to manufacturing exports) are experiencing labor shortages. This has led to improved working conditions and higher wages in many factories located in these regions.[52] Chinese manufacturers in Guangdong (Pearl River Delta) and Fujian (which lies between the Pearl River Delta and the Yangtze River Delta) are experiencing a worker shortage of about two million workers.[53] China is not running out of workers, but factories are being forced to pay more and offer better living conditions. In part this is a result of the explosive growth of the economy and in part it can be attributed to the success of family planning. For the next fifteen years the number of workers entering the workforce will gradually decline. To attract workers some cities are raising the minimum wage and manufacturers are offering improved working conditions. Workers are also becoming more informed—using the internet, text messaging and email to compare their wages with the wages in other parts of the country.

Vietnam, India, and Bangladesh, among other countries, now have lower wage costs than China. The 2004 article from the *Independent* telling the story of Warmi predicted that because of the expiration of the Multi-Fiber Agreement Indonesia and Bangladesh would lose one million jobs and there would be substantial losses in Cambodia, Mexico, Nepal, and Kenya as well. It predicted that China, and possibly India and Pakistan, would gain jobs. Even as these predictions were being made, apparently unbeknownst to the authors, the first worker shortages were being reported in Chinese papers. In the mid-2000s job losses were happening in Indonesia, in many places in Africa, and the Americas, but the situation is fluid and it is hard to predict which country will gain or lose textile jobs.

Against *The Independent*'s prediction, Cambodia did not lose jobs even though it is not usually listed among the countries possessing wage advantages vis-a-vis China. Working together with the ILO, Cambodia set up labor unions and closely monitored workers' rights to ensure that workers receive a living wage. Cambodia marketed itself as a country that prohibits sweatshops. In 2005, even with the end of the Multi-Fiber Agreement, sixteen new clothing plants opened in Cambodia and this more than replaced the twelve factories that failed.[54] Thirty thousand new jobs were created and even though price pressure may have contributed to the failure of wages to keep up with inflation, the average wage of $72.00 per month in clothing factories was well above Cambodia's minimum wage of $45.00 a month.[55] The case of Cambodia suggests that the demand for living wages and acceptable working conditions, prudently applied, can actually save jobs in some circumstances. In 2013–14 garment workers in Cambodia pushed for higher wages and the ouster of the country's longtime leader. It is difficult to protest in countries where the freedom to do so is not respected. When local workers do go out on strike, at considerable risk to themselves, I think we who buy the clothes they produce should look for ways to support them. I am not sure exactly how we do that, but perhaps the key is to make it clear to clothing manufacturers that we do care about the conditions under which our clothes are made.

Many companies are claiming to be concerned about the working conditions of those who stitch their clothes, and consumers should indicate that they too care about labor conditions. The GAP website tells of its efforts in China to ensure workers' rights. It has encouraged factories to form workers committees to monitor working conditions in the factories. GAP states emphatically that it holds its factories in China to the same standards that it holds all of its other factories to. It is possible that some who argue for labor standards are merely looking for ways to protect industries that are no longer competitive in the world market. We should ask what people in the affected countries are saying. If, as was the case in the Indonesian factory owned by Dae Joo, the workers themselves are asking for redress, then we should support them.

One of the most serious impediments to labor rights in China is the hukou system, which restricts workers' movement from the country to the cities. This system originated in the 1950s and was designed to keep the great majority of citizens in rural areas. Beginning in the late 1980s the system was modified to allow workers into the manufacturing zones.[56] The system is currently undergoing further modification, as China is planning to move large numbers of its rural population to cities in an effort to reduce poverty and spur domestic consumption. Even with this liberalization, rural workers working outside their hukou do not have full rights. They are accorded a special status and are called roughly "floating people." They work 25 percent more hours a week, but earn 40 percent less than those that are registered in urban areas.[57] By limiting the options of workers, the Chinese state helps to keep the cost of labor down and to stem the flow of people from the country to the city, but the cost to the workers is often high. For example, Zheng Quingming was a poor high school student from a rural area of Sichuan Province who killed himself because he was not allowed to sit for the college entrance exam. He owed $80 in school fees—probably less than a wealthy urban Chinese citizen might pay for a cell phone.[58] Quingming's story graphically illustrates serious problems lurking behind the Chinese miracle. China reported that in 2003, the number of destitute poor, which the Chinese government defines as those making less than the equivalent of $75 a year, grew by 800,000 to 85 million Chinese in total. The disparity in income between rural and urban Chinese is among the greatest in the world, and for a long time the hukou laws rarely allowed rural dwellers access to the urban areas. Quingming's pursuit of a college education is understandable given that it is one of the few legal avenues leading from the country into the city. Those who emigrate illegally from the countryside to the city are subject to the kinds of pressures that undocumented workers face worldwide. As we have already said, China is in the process of modifying the system and it is now encouraging rural residents to migrate to the cities. By 2020 the government wants 250 million rural people to migrate to the cities, although it is trying to get them to migrate to smaller cities (with less than 5 million). It is even planning to give 100 million of these migrants a full hukou for these cities.[59] India is also faced with the problem of how to distribute wealth from the prosperous urban areas to the less prosperous countryside. China's hukou system has largely prevented the massive slums that are found in India, but I would still be hard-pressed to endorse a system that imposes less than full citizenship status on its internal migrants. Unlike China the population of India has a chance to voice its dissent in elections. In the global South the majority of humanity lives in rural areas and it is important for countries to find ways to manage the massive migrations to the cities. Ideally this would take the form of incentives to stay in the rural areas as well as helping the migrants navigate the journey as opposed to prohibitions.

In *Travels of a T-Shirt in the Global Economy*, Pietra Rivoli describes the history of the textile industry as a "long race to the bottom."[60] She argues that the production of cotton textiles led to the industrial revolution in Great Britain and then the United States. The industry has looked for young women who were perceived to be more docile than men since its inception. As the workers organized and demanded better wages, the factories tended to move to places where labor was cheaper: from England to New England, to the southern United States and then to Japan (where textiles flourished from about 1890 to 1960). After Japan, Hong Kong in the mid-1970s became the world's largest textile manufacturer and now the mantle has past to China. Rivoli argues that the cotton mill and the sweatshop were the impetus for the development of "urbanization, industrialization, and economic diversification . . . as well as the economic and social liberation of women from the farm."[61] Even though she believes that the mills have brought progress, she also argues that governments, labor unions, religious leaders, and international organizations have all had a part in making the working conditions in sweat shops more bearable. Thanks to textile machinery, "missing fingers, hands, arms and legs were so common a sight in Manchester, England, that Friedrich Engels likened Manchester to a place soldiers returned to after war."[62] Reformers made the industry a more humane place to work. She chronicles how working conditions have improved for many workers in the United States, and now even in China working conditions are improving.

Rivoli argues that reformers have a role to play and there is much evidence as well as many stories that document the truly brutal circumstances in which many labor. The 2013 collapse of the Rana Plaza building in Bangladesh in which 1,127 people died tragically underlined how first world demand is linked to suffering in faraway places. Most reformers are not asking the companies to boycott places like Bangladesh, but instead to work with their suppliers to insure better treatment of workers. According to the *New York Times*, Chinese workers who produce for the U.S. market are suffering from "a surge in fatal respiratory, circulatory, neurological and digestive tract diseases like those American workers suffered at the dawn of the industrial age."[63] To illustrate the problem the article tells the story of Hu Zhiguo, a forty-four-year-old worker who is dying from silicosis, a respiratory disease that he contracted from making cheap jewelry from iridescent stones like opal, topaz, and malachite. The factory installed improved ventilation after the first cases of the disease appeared, but an inspection in the summer of 2002 by Huizhou Center for Disease Control revealed that some work stations, even with the new ventilation system "had ambient silica concentrations as high as 70 times the standard allowed by the Chinese safety code, which is less strict than related American and European standards by a factor of twenty."[64] And if that is not graphic enough, the article uses another illustration. Mr. Hu has inhaled more quartz dust in ten years than China's safety standards would permit in a thousand. Apparently there are still ways to get around the problem. The plant owner rejected the results of last summer's inspection and arranged for another inspection by a different agency, which it passed. No longer able to work, after a long legal battle, Mr. Hu received a onetime $25,000 dollar settlement from his employer. He has used most of that up. He returned to his hometown and opened up a store. He turned it over to his wife because he no longer has the strength to work, and now his sixteen-year-old son will have to quit high school and find a job to help support the family.

Markets are always shaped by regulations. The success of the Asian tigers suggests that governments that take an active role in shaping their development leave their citizens much better off than governments that are too laissez-faire or repressive. Global poverty is not just a question of how much we the wealthy should give to help the poor. The story of Mr. Hu graphically highlights the ruined lives that often stand behind the products and services that we buy. Be it the makers of jewelry, or hamburgers, be it those who clean our offices, sell us products from Walmart, or sew our clothes, much of the life of even the moderately wealthy is made possible in part by the work of the poor and much of the labor of the poor remains hidden from us. It is hard to know under what conditions the laborers work who produce the myriad of things we use in our everyday lives. We consume so much and it comes from all over the world, but we should seek out ways to ensure that those who are making the things we use are not being ruthlessly exploited.

We should become informed consumers and be attuned to the nuances of each situation. Let me give just one more example to show how important it is to find a nuanced response. Flowers are often given to show one's appreciation, but what is the cost of producing flowers? Imported flowers must be free of insects and disease, and in order to meet these standards "growers rely on heavy use of toxic pesticides, fungicides and other chemicals."[65] It has been reported that 20 percent of the chemicals used in the South have been shown to be dangerous and are restricted or banned in Europe and North America.[66] The work itself is also often difficult. Workers must often kneel on the ground to plant the seedlings. Finally, there is the danger of environmental hazards from the chemicals, either from runoff into streams or from local people recycling containers and plastic sheeting used in the greenhouses. The International Labor Organization studies the flower-growing industry in Colombia and reported that there is a group of large, well-established flower growers who treat their workers in compliance with local laws.[67] The report concludes, however, that the smaller flower farms compete with the larger farms by paying lower wages. Finally, there is a third group of flower producers who rely on subcontractors for their workers. In these enterprises that rely solely on subcontracted workers, the ILO found that social security benefits, occupational risk insurance, and family compensation funds are rarely found. Precisely because there are different types of enterprises involved in the growing of flowers, it is difficult to generalize about the industry as a whole. Wholesale generalizations that the industry is treating its workers well ignore the working conditions of the majority of contracted workers. Calls to boycott the flowers of Colombia would hurt the firms that are treating their workers well, but consumer pressure is indubitably one of the factors that contribute to improving working conditions for some workers. And not all workers are being treated well. Even though much of what we use in our daily lives is produced or grown by people who live in desperate poverty, the ILO report about the varied conditions within the Colombian flower industry drives home the importance of a nuanced response. What we need is help in identifying those enterprises that treat their workers well.

FAIR TRADE

Buying fair trade products is one way to try to insure that those who produce the things we buy are treated fairly. I like to start my day with a good cup of coffee. I am not alone. The international trade in coffee represents more than $55 billion a year. I have been known to pay more than $2.00 for a cup at my local coffee shop and more than $12.00 a pound from a mail-order house in San Francisco. That Sumartran is really good! The laborers who grow and pick the coffee are often lucky to have $2.00 a day on which to live. We live in a strange world. Some of us spend on a single cup of coffee what almost half the world has to spend on everything they need for an entire day. Many in the world have next to nothing—not enough to eat, not even clean water— even as some of the world's poor produce many of the goods we consume every day. Like many I try to keep my weight down and prevent heart disease by jogging. The World Health Organization reported that there are approximately 170 million children in poor countries that are underweight because of lack of food, "while more than a billion adults in the United States, Europe and middle income countries are thought to be obese or overweight."[68] In doing my best to reduce the number of overweight by one, I buy (somewhat) expensive sneakers for my three-times-a-week jog. Who sews my shoes and how much do they make? I would not knowingly buy a product made with slave labor, but by several accounts I am buying products that are made by workers who may not be making a living wage.

If we have earned the $200,000 our house costs, are we entitled to live in it? If we have earned the money to buy a car—or at least we have earned enough for the monthly payments—are we entitled to drive one? Given that we earned the $250 that it costs to take ourselves and our significant other out to the Ritz-Carlton, are we entitled to that meal? Have we have earned the right to pay $2.00 for a cup of "good" coffee, or $80 for a pair of sneakers, if we are buying a product that was made by someone who earns less than a living wage?

Coffee, along with alcohol, is one of the last legal drugs—small wonder, given that it is the perfect drug to keep workers alert on their jobs. Worldwide coffee prices fluctuate widely. A few years ago Vietnam started to sell large amounts of coffee on the world markets and that produced a glut in supply. Prices dropped. Many farmers were receiving less per pound than it cost to grow the beans. Coffee beans were literally being left to rot on the bushes. Small farmers were particularly hard-hit. In some countries land reform has made it possible for some farmers to own their own land. Some of these small farmers are losing everything that they have spent their life to accumulate. Many small farmers have worked for years eating little else but rice and beans while trying to make a living out of growing coffee. Even in good years it is difficult to be a small farmer. As I write this, prices have recovered, but if we are looking for ways to ensure that those who labor on our behalf receive living wages then we should consider buying fair trade products. Fair trade eliminates middlemen and pays the farmer a guaranteed price to ensure the growers of the crop have received a living wage. The extra money that fair trade brings is also used to improve the crops, and half of the extra money is used to promote education, health and clean water.

One could argue that buying fair trade is just a drop in the bucket, but in fact the idea seems to be catching on. The United States has seen a remarkable growth in the number of companies offering fair trade certified products. In 1999 only 33 companies did this, while in 2002, 160 companies were offering these products. Today one finds fair trade products everywhere, including at our local supermarkets. Fair trade coffee is also sold on more than two hundred campuses nationwide.[69] Starbucks bought 2.1 million pounds of fair trade coffee in 2003, 4.8 million pounds in 2004 and 39 million pounds in 2009. They seem to be buying slightly less fair trade coffee now, but they claim that 95 percent of their coffee is "ethically sourced." Dunkin' Donuts uses fair trade coffee in all of its premium coffee drinks. This is a movement that is not just limited to coffee. One can now buy fair trade soccer balls, clothes, wine, olive oil, spices, nuts, cotton, juice, and chocolate, as well as fresh fruit and vegetables. Fair trade cooperatives assure that no forced or child labor is used.[70] The majority of those helped out small farms. The cooperatives are democratically managed, nondiscriminating, and encourage environmental protection. The fair trade premium is used for the social and economic benefit of the members.[71]

In a similar vein, some rugs come with certificates that claim they have not been made by child labor. My children's soccer balls were made in Pakistan and have a claim written on them that child labor was not used to produce them. This may be false advertising, and it may not even be a gain for children, but the fact that these products are so labeled is a sign that many consumers do worry about the conditions under which the products they buy are produced. Once people agree to the principle that workers should receive a living wage, it will be necessary to set up the mechanisms to assure that claims about labor conditions are indeed true and that the reforms are made in ways that really do help workers.

The fair trade designation promises accountability, and a way to distinguish between products coming from farmers who are receiving a living wage and those who are not. I am not at all averse to paying extra to insure that the people who grow my food or make the things that I buy are treated well. I really don't want to wear clothes that are produced by laborers who are not making a living wage. I don't want to give flowers or chocolate that is literally killing or enslaving the workers who are growing them. These are fairly uncontroversial positions. And I think that there are many others who feel the same way. What we need is help figuring out which producers are treating their workers fairly. Fair trade offers a gradual transformation. This promises less dislocation than a top-down command or a boycott. As consumers demand fair trade products, producers can shift production. Those of us who want to buy products that are produced by workers making a living wage should support such initiatives.

Our supermarkets are chock-full of products from around the world. There are intense debates about the effects of globalization, but like it or not we are increasingly living in a world that is interconnected. The food on our tables and the tables themselves are very likely to be produced somewhere halfway across the world. Do we want to buy products—coffee, clothes, shoes, jewelry, or for that matter, hamburgers that are produced by people who are not making living wages? Particularly when we have the option, why not look for products that we know are produced by companies that pay

people a living wage? I am not suggesting that we buy only products produced by workers who make as much as well-paid workers in the United
States. I am only arguing that if we have the opportunity and it does not pose
a significant burden, then we should seek out and promote products that are
produced by workers who receive a living wage. Exactly what constitutes a
living wage will vary greatly from place to place. Clearly, workers in the
United States need to earn more than workers in Haiti because it costs more
to live in the United States.

In addition to the ethical arguments for buying fair trade, there are other
more self-interested reasons, particularly in the case of food, to buy products
from people who have received living wages. If profit margins are cut to the
bone, producers may resort to unsafe practices. In the 2008 milk scandal in
China, for example, melamine was added to milk in part because farmers
were under intense pressure to sell milk cheaply. Three hundred thousand
people were affected, and several children even died. In the United States in
2009, six people were killed by tainted peanut butter.[72] Insuring that farmers
and the rest of the steps in the food supply chain receive a living wage takes
away some of the pressure to cheat.

Fair trade is merely one way to try to insure that those who labor on our
behalf receive a fair wage. Once we establish that workers should receive
living wages we can look for a variety of mechanisms to ensure that they do.
Consumers have long paid for the prestige of wearing designer labels; many
may very well pay for humane treatment of workers. The actions of companies show that they are concerned about the public perception of their business practices. Most major companies have detailed reports on their websites
about their programs to protect the workers who produce their goods. According to one report, already in 2000, 85 percent of all large companies in
the United States had such written policies.[73] For example, GAP has a thirty-
page report on its website detailing its relationship with its suppliers. Nike,
Reebok and even Walmart have such statements as well. Whereas GAP,
Nike, and Reebok hire independent inspectors for their overseas factories,
Walmart inspectors work for the company.

Consumer demand for goods produced in accordance with international
labor standards is a market-based solution. The solution may be at times to
boycott the products of exploited labor, but it may be more effective to help
create a market for those producers that treat their employees well. Medea
Benjamin of Global Exchange argues that Nike could guarantee all of its
workers in Indonesia a living wage by diverting less than 3 percent of its
advertising budget.[74] These wage increases could also be paid by very modest increases in the price of the products, and surveys have suggested that
consumers would be willing to pay a bit more to insure that workers receive a
living wage. According to one survey, 86 percent of Americans would be
willing to pay an extra dollar for an article costing $20 to assure that the

article was not produced in a sweatshop.[75] A more recent study also found that consumers in New York City were willing to pay more for candles and towels that were by made by workers when it was advertised that the workers had been treated fairly and with dignity.[76]

In response to numerous criticisms, Nike has made many changes including raising the minimum age for workers in its shoe factories to eighteen and raising the minimum age of workers in its apparel, accessories and equipment factories to sixteen. Nike has also started to pay workers in Indonesia that country's minimum wage. It had avoided doing this before 1996 by applying every year for an exemption to the Indonesian minimum wage law.[77] Nike has posted on its web site a section on workers and factories where it promises to monitor closely the conditions throughout its system of production. Nike cites two, NGOs Fair Labor Association and Global Alliance for Workers and Communities, as partners that help it to monitor working conditions. It is hard to judge to what extent these companies are actually complying with their codes of conduct, but the very fact that they have such codes speaks to the concern they have that significant numbers of consumers will not buy the products of sweatshop labor.

A LIVING WAGE IN THE UNITED STATES

The United States has the worst inequality of any wealthy nation and many of the poor work either directly or indirectly for the rich.[78] According to the Economic Policy Institute, a living wage in the United States for a family of one adult and two children is about $30,000 and 60 percent of U.S. citizens make beneath that.[79] In other words, the study argues that the majority of workers in the United States may not be receiving wages and benefits that allow them basic shelter, health care, child care and food. Walmart, the largest employer in the United States, has suffered under an avalanche of bad publicity regarding its treatment of workers. On October 23, 2003, federal agents rounded up 250 illegal immigrants in sixty of its stores in twenty-one different states. A lawyer who has sued Walmart on behalf of the immigrant janitors estimated that Walmart used thousands of illegal immigrants to clean more than one thousand of its stores.[80] It has been reported that these illegal immigrants worked 7 days a week—364 days of the year—for below minimum wages. The workers were hired by subcontractors and Walmart claims that its senior management did not know about the practice, but that has been disputed by several individuals who claim that they contacted Walmart to complain about the treatment of the illegal immigrant janitors.[81] It settled the case by paying a record fine of $11 million, which is four times larger than any other fine ever paid to the government in an illegal immigrant employment case—but a miniscule amount when one considers how much the company makes! Apparently, Walmart is not the only one doing this. Target also settled a lawsuit brought by the U.S. government that alleged that it had undocumented workers cleaning its stores for wages that were far below minimum wage.[82] Those of us who would criticize China for its hukou system should also work to reform the system that allows undocumented workers in the United States to be exploited while they harvest our food, clean our stores, tend to our yards, cook our food and clean our homes.

Given Walmart's recent troubles and its position as the United States' leading private employer it is a particularly visible target, but it is far from the only problematic employer and probably not the worst. It has been reported that "modern-day slaves toil in Florida's fields of plenty."[83] According to the *Palm Beach Post* some farm workers reported being locked up, raped, struck by lightning, sickened by pesticides and shorted on pay to the point that they could barely survive. Housing is often abominable. In Palm Beach County there is licensed migrant housing for only 6,635 workers, but the paper estimates that during the season there are between 20,000–45,000 workers. In addition to the farm workers, there are undocumented women who are lured into prostitution in "21 Clubs" where men buy sex for $20 and a condom for $1.

Many documented workers have a very hard time surviving on the wages Walmart pays. Barbara Ehrenreich explains in *Nickel and Dimed: On Not Getting By in America* that she was not able to make ends meet on a Walmart salary even though she had a car, did not pay for health insurance, and did not have any children to support. She also told the stories of how difficult it was for others working there to survive on their salaries. *The Atlanta Journal-Constitution* reported that more than 10,000 dependents of employees of Walmart relied on the State of Georgia on the state-sponsored health insurance. Walmart is the largest employer in the state, but the next-largest employer had only 734 of its employees' dependents on the program. This is consistent with Ehrenreich's recent report that more than half of Walmart employees cannot afford the company's health insurance.[84] It has been reported that more than half of Walmart workers with children live below the poverty line.[85] Other big discount retailers treat their workers better. Ehrenreich contrasts Walmart to Costco, another large retailer, where 90 percent of its employees have company-provided health care. Clearly, Walmart is concerned about its image. At times Walmart has run advertisements on public television and on National Public Radio claiming that Walmart offers opportunities for career advancement and supports local communities and businesses. As I have just recounted, there is plenty of evidence to the contrary, but the advertisement is a telling sign of where the company believes its public relations problems lie.

What does it say about the United States, the wealthiest nation in the world, that its largest private employer pays so many of its workers non-living wages? What does it say about the United States that there are many reports about how undocumented workers are exploited to provide basic services such as harvesting our food and cleaning our stores? If this is what we have learned to tolerate in our own country, is it not surprising that we tolerate exploitation of workers in other countries who are also working to make our lives possible. There is no question that someone living under a dollar a day is much worse off than an undocumented worker cleaning a Walmart or Target store, but the fact that so many workers in the United States are so poorly paid tells us a great deal about our ability to live with injustice even when it is very close to home. Do I really want to shop at a retailer that exploits undocumented workers and doesn't pay its documented sales force a living wage? Why not look for retailers with a higher standard of ethics? The case for doing so is particularly strong when there are easily accessible alternatives that treat their workers better. I would not fault anyone who is struggling to feed themselves for shopping at Walmart, but those of us who have better options should turn to them.

Walmart argues that its low prices help those who are poor, but at what cost to its workers? Some argue that Walmart plays a crucial role in employing those who would not qualify for higher-paying jobs. This may be true, but these people still need basic necessities to live. If Walmart does not provide them with health care, someone must and isn't it an unfair competitive advantage to allow Walmart to shift health care to the state while other companies pay it? If we continue to allow Walmart and other large retailers in the United States to pay non-living wages, it is hard to fault other companies who are trying to compete with Walmart that also pay non-living wages. By allowing companies to pay non-living wages we are inviting the exploitation of workers. It stands as a stunning testimony to much of what is wrong in the United States that its largest employer pays so many so poorly. I am not sure how best to improve the lot of the Walmart worker and other low-paid workers, but failure to provide a living wage is not a morally acceptable option.

Given the choice, I think many people are willing to pay a bit more to insure that workers receive a living wage. The reason that the living wage movement has not gone further than it has is that we are often ignorant of the plight of others. It is much easier to accept the status quo when we have no direct knowledge of the suffering of others. It is all too easy to overlook the human cost that has gone into growing and harvesting crops, cooking our food, making our clothes, and building and maintaining the structures in which we live and work. To the extent that we are ignorant of the suffering of the world it is easy to ignore it, but the more we become aware of the conditions under which the poor toil to make our life possible, the easier it is to see that we really ought to do something about it.

What do we owe those who make the shoes on our feet, sew the shirt on our back, and grow and harvest the food we put in our belly? How much do we owe to those who cook and serve us our food? Charity is, finally, a small part of the ethics of poverty. Krugman is right to warn us about naive remedies, but it is incumbent upon all of us who live off the work of others and benefit from the current world economic order to address the conditions under which the poor work and live. We should work to change the multiple systems that privilege the wealthy and exploit the poor. We should work to change international agreements that unduly benefit the wealthy and well connected. We should support initiatives like fair trade that endeavor to insure that workers earn a living wage. We owe those who labor, particularly those who labor on our behalf, a living wage. In addition, we should join with others to stop the exploitation that all too often accompanies the extraction of minerals. In doing all of these things we will not only benefit the poor, but we may very well be making our own lives more secure.

Problems are much easier to see than to solve. Even middle-class lives rely on the exploitation of others. We need to build coalitions with the exploited to bring about a more just global economic system. Some things seem obvious such as buying fair trade products and eliminating agricultural subsidies to big agribusiness. Other steps are more controversial such as Pogge's call for a tax on minerals. Such a tax doesn't seem like a bad idea to me, but as a philosopher I am not very well qualified to judge the likely efficacy of such measures. My goal has been to point out the ethical problems in the way we are living now. We cannot begin to correct these problems unless those whose lives we are trying to ameliorate play an active role in envisioning and making the changes. Together we can think about what exactly would be the most effective actions to reduce the savage poverty under which so many in this world suffer.

NOTES

1. Charles W. Mills argues that discussion around global poverty should be viewed as discussions of rectificatory as opposed to distributive justice. I agree with Mills that any full account of justice must consider the historical wrongs including slavery and colonialism. See "Realizing (Through Racializing) Pogge" in *Thomas Pogge and His Critics*. pp 151-174. As we will see, there is also plenty of evidence that people are being harmed today so that I might drive my car, cool my house, and surf the net.

2. The interconnectedness of the world and the moral implications of this interconnectedness has been recognized for a very long time. More than twenty-five years ago Charles R. Beitz argued that the interconnectedness of the world raises serious doubts about Rawls' attempts to understand justice primarily within national borders. As Beitz notes, even Kant recognized that once international trade is established, justice becomes an international rather than a merely national concern. See his "Justice and International Relations" in *International Ethics* ed. Beitz, Cohen, Scanlon and Simmons (Princeton: Princeton University Press, 1985) p.283.

3. Nicholas Shaxson. *Poisoned Wells: The Dirty Politics of African Oil* (Pelgrave: New York, 2007) p. 194.

4. http://money.cnn.com/2008/01/02/markets/oil/index.htm?postversion=2008010212

5. Peter Maas *Crude World: The Violent Twilight of Oil,* (Vintage: New York, 2009) p. 84

6. To see Chevron's side of the story, go to its website where you will find a long, detailed account: http://www.chevron.com/ecuador/background/patternoffraud/. To get another version of the events see Amnesty International: http://www.amnestyusa.org/business-and-human-rights/extractives/chevron-corp/page.do?id=1101670.

7. John Ghazvinian, *Untapped: The Scramble for Africa's Oil* (Orlando: Harcourt, 2007) p. 132.

8. Peter Singer makes this point in *The Life You Can Save* p. 31. Thomas Pogge makes it also in many places, among them "Assisting the Global Poor" in *The Ethics of Assistance* ed. Deen K. Chatterjee (Cambridge: Cambridge University Press, 2007, pp. 260-288. Joshua Cohen argues that Pogge's solution to this and other problems associated with global poverty relies too much on finding a just global institutional order. Cohen downplays the role of the international order in the resource curse. Nigeria, Angola, and Equatorial Guinea seem to me to make the case for Pogge's claim, especially in the case of mineral wealth, that the problem must be addressed by global institutional reform. As long as ruling elites have oil wealth, it proves very hard to dislodge them. See Cohen's "Philosophy, Social Science and Global Poverty" in *Thomas Pogge and His Critics* ed. Alison Jaggar (Cambridge UK: Polity, 2010) pp. 18-45.

9. Ghazvinian, *Untapped: The Scramble for Africa's Oil* 135-6.

10. http://www.globalwitness.org/library/gaps-angolas-official-oil-revenue-data-undermine-transparency-new-report-finds

11. See Macartan Humphreys, Jeffrey D. Sachs & Joseph Stiglitz editors, *Escaping the Resource Curse* (New York: Columbia University Press, 2007) p. 25.

12. "After China's Rare Earth Embargo, A New Calculus," *New York Times*, 29 October, 2010.

13. http://www.rfa.org/english/news/china_pollution-20080222.html

14. "How Congress Devastated Congo," *New York Times*, 7 August 2011 p. A19.

15. Ryszard Kapuscinski as quoted in *Crude World: The Violent Twilight of Oil.* 159.

16. *The Idea of Justice*, 173.

17. See, for example, the study cited by Humphreys et al that found a correlation between oil and coal production and gubernatorial turnover. When governments are not as reliant on their citizens for the revenue to run the states, it should not surprise us that politicians are less attuned to their citizens' demands. *Escaping the Resource Curse*, p. 12.

18. See *World Poverty and Human Rights* 162-66 and "Response to the Critics" in *Thomas Pogge and His Critics* pp. 227-228.

19. Cohen raises these questions in "Philosophy, Social Science, Global Poverty" and Pogge replies in "Response to the Critics"; both are found in *Thomas Pogge and His Critics*.

20. Sen *The Idea of Justice*, p. 263.

21. Singer has written a book about how Henry Spira pressured corporations to reduce the amount of animal cruelty. See Peter Singer, *Ethics into Action: Henry Spira and the Animal Rights Movement* (Lanham MD: Rowman & Littlefield, 2000).

22. Joseph Stiglitz, *Globalization and Its Discontents* (New York: Norton, 2003); Joseph E. Stiglitz and Andrew Charlton, *Fair Trade for All: How Trade Can Promote Development* (Oxford: Oxford University Press, 2005); Joseph Stiglitz, *Making Globalization Work.* (New York: Norton, 2006).

23. A defense of the IMF is offered by Stanley Fisher. See his *IMF Essays from a Time of Crisis: The International Financial System, Stabilization, and Development* (Cambridge: The MIT Press 2004). I am grateful to Grant Stewart, a student of mine at Georgia College & State University who made me aware of this book.

24. Stiglitz, 93. Paul Krugman wrote a now famous article in support of Malaysia's decision "Saving Asia, it is Time to get Radical" (*Fortune* Magazine 9/7/98). Stanley Fischer, former First Managing Director of the International Monetary Fund, writes a fairly warm response to the Malaysian decision. Amusingly referring only to the fact that certain "leading academics"

agreed with Malaysia, he does not confront the critics of the IMF policy in detail. He argues that most countries have not responded as Malaysia has by applying controls—which is a very poor argument which may very well say more about the power of the IMF than the success of the policy. Second Fisher argues that "most advanced countries have fully liberalized capital flows." Again, the fact that many have done it does not make it right and it is not clear that the economic policies that work for large nations will work for smaller ones. For Fischer's views see his *IMF Essays from a Time of Crisis: The International Financial System, Stabilization, and Development* (Cambridge: The MIT Press, 2004) p. 147.

25. See *A Fair Globalization: Creating Opportunities for All: An ILO Report prepared by the World Commission on the Social Dimensions of Globalization* (Geneva, Switzerland: 2004) p. 29.

26. Stiglitz, *Globalization and Its Discontents*, p. 97.

27. Stiglitz, *Globalization and Its Discontents*, p. 97.

28. Stiglitz 112-113

29. See *Fair Trade for All* p. 225. Stiglitz and Charlton cite a 2003 study by K. Anderson "How Can Agricultural Trade Reform Reduce Poverty" Centre for International Economic Studies, University of Adelaide, Discussion Paper 0323 that makes this argument.

30. Peter Singer and Jim Mason, *The Ethics of What We Eat* (Rodale, 2006) p. 155.

31. http://omiusajpic.org/wp-content/uploads/2008/02/paying_the_price.pdf An earlier study estimated that the effect would be less. http://www.aaec.ttu.edu/ceri/Published%20Papers/Journal%20Article/TheImpactsUSCtnPrgWldMkt.pdf

32. Stiglitz, *Making Globalization Work*, 85-6.

33. *New York Times* "Subsidies Rest on What Kind of Row You Hoe". 18 Feb. 2005

34. *New York Times* "Sugar Industry Lobby Loses Some Luster Over Stance on Trade" 2 June 2005. *New York Times* "American Candy Makers, Pinched by Inflated Sugar Prices, Look Abroad" 30 October 2013

35. Peter Singer *The Life You Can Save*, p. 114.

36. "US and Brazil Reach Agreement on Cotton Dispute," *New York Times*, 6 April 2010.

37. http://www.depts.ttu.edu/ceri/Default.aspx. I thank Darren Hudson for making me aware of some of the complexities surrounding these tariffs. To see his take, which is in many ways at odds with mine, see his blog: http://agcompetitiveness.blogspot.com/2010/04/brazil-and-cotton-part-deux.html

38. Richard W. Miller argues that wealthy nations have unfairly taken advantage of poorer nations and that as a result they have a responsibility to change these trade arrangements and make up for the injustice they have caused. Realizing that new and more equitable trade arrangements will adversely affect some of the most vulnerable citizens of wealthy countries, Miller argues that wealthy countries should take steps to help their citizens that are adversely affected by these new trade arrangements. Wealthy countries should not make poor countries shoulder the burden of protecting vulnerable people in wealthy countries. See his *Globalizing Justice: The Ethics of Poverty and Power* chapter 3.

39. See Stiglitz and Charlton, *Fair Trade for All* p. 24.

40. Ibid.

41. Stiglitz, *Making Globalization Work*, 65-66.

42. Dan Twining "An Indian election primer" *Foreign Policy*, 16 April 2009.

43. Pogge and Cohen debate this point. Cohen does not argue against the removal of agricultural subsidies, but believes that Pogge overstates the impact such a removal would have (*Thomas Pogge and His Critics*, 27). Pogge responds by citing several studies that back his claim that the removal of trade barriers, including agricultural subsidies and import restrictions, would indeed lead to large-scale reductions in the number of people living in poverty around the world. Among the studies he cites are the United Nations Conference on Trade and Development report "*Fragile Recovery and Risks* (New York: UN Publications 1999), IX (also available at www.unctad.org/en/docs/tdr1999_enpdf.) Pogge also cites Santiago Fernandez de Córdoba and David Vanzetti, "Now What? Searching for a solution to the WTO Industrial Tariff Negotiations," in Sam Laird and Santiago Fernandez de Córdoba (eds), *Coping with Trade Reforms: A Developing-Country Perspective on the WTO Industrial Tariff Negotiations* (Basingstoke: Palgrave Macmillan, 2006). They argue that reforms in global trade would lead

to a $135.3 billion gain for less developed countries. He also cites William R. Cline, *Trade Policy and Global Poverty* (Washington DC: Center for Global Development, 2004), who argues that these reforms would lead to a direct gain of more than $86 billion and a $203 billion gain when one figures in the productivity gains. Pogge also cites a World Bank Report *Global Economic Prospects 2002* (Washington, DC: World Bank, 2002) that projects that 320 million people could be lifted out of poverty by these reforms. Pogge and Cohen agree that reforms must be measured to judge their effectiveness. Pogge's position is also supported by Stiglitz's work.

44. See its website www.ilo.org

45. See Maria C. Mattioli and V.K. Sapovadia "Laws of Labor: Core Labor Standards and Global Trade" *Harvard International Review* vol. xxvi, no. 2, summer 2004. p. 64.

46. "In Praise of Cheap Labor: Bad jobs are better than no jobs at all." *Slate* March 20, 1997. For a philosophical discussion of the ethical issues surrounding the things we buy, see David T. Schwartz's fine book *Consuming Choices: Ethics in a Global Consumer World* (Lanham: Rowman & Littlefield, 2010).

47. Eric V. Edmonds, "Does Child Labor Decline with Improving Economic Status?", *Journal of Human Resources*, vol. 40, no. 1, 2005. See also Edmonds' study "The Effect of Trade Liberalization on Child Labor," *Journal of International Economics* 2005.

48. Even if it makes sense for the individual family there are good arguments for the prohibition of child labor. The use of cheap labor lessens the incentive for companies to invest in new technologies. And, as we have already said, child labor also deprives children of an education and therefore is a drag on the development of a nation's labor force. An educated labor force is in turn an important factor in attracting direct foreign investment to a country. Child labor often leaves children physically disabled and unable to support themselves as adults. The Harkin bill is well-intentioned, but it highlights the dangers of quick fixes. Economic prescriptions need to give those affected, particularly when the affected are vulnerable such as children and the very poor, the time and the means to adjust. See Maria C. Mattioli and V.K. Sapovadia "Laws of Labor: Core Labor Standards and Global Trade" *Harvard International Review* vol. xxvi, no. 2, summer 2004. p. 62.

49. "US Agency to Be Cited in Suit About Trade and Child Labor" *New York Times* 29 May 2003. There have been other reports in the *New York Times* of slave labor used in the harvesting of wood (the wood is destined for the making of furniture for export) in Brazil. The *Times* told a story about Bernardo Gomes da Silvia who was held in virtual slavery for 12 years receiving no wages as he was forced to work from 6 in the morning to at times 11 p.m. These labor practices are used by some in the beef and timber industries primarily to supply exports. A group called the Pastoral Land Commission affiliated with the Roman Catholic Church estimates that the number of slave laborers in Brazil is increasing. It believes there were 25,000 such workers in 2002 whereas a decade earlier it estimates that there were 5,000. "Brazil's Prized Exports Rely On Slaves and Scorched Land," *New York Times,* 26 March 2002. The BBC reported that some of the workers who were working on projects related to the 2014 World Cup were working under "slave like conditions." "Brazil World Cup Workers Face Slave Like Conditions" 9/26/2013 http://www.bbc.com/news/world-latin-america-24292174

50. "Stitched up: the human cost of cheap clothing," *The Independent* 27 July 2004

51. These statistics are from a 2004 Conference Board Study and are quoted in Pietra Rivoli's *Travels of a T-Shirt in the Global Economy: An Economist Examines the Markets, Power and Politics of the World* (Wiley, New York, 2005) p.227, no. 4.

52. See "Sharp Labor Shortage in China May Lead to World Trade Shift" *New York Times,* 3 April 2006.

53. "Help Wanted: China Finds Itself with a Labor Shortage," *New York Times,* 3 April 2005.

54. See "Low Cost and Sweatshop Free: Cambodia Garment Makers Hold Off a Vast Chinese Challenge," *New York Times,* 12 May 2005.

55. See ILO report "Cambodian Garment Industry One Year Later."

56. *Travels of a T-Shirt* 89.

57. Ibid. Rivoli quotes this statistic from Wang, Feng and Xuejin Zuo "Inside China's Cities: Institutional Barriers and Opportunities for Urban Migrants. " *American Economic Review* 89, no. 2, 1999, pp. 276-280.

58. "Amid China's Boom, No Helping Hand for Young Qingming" *New York* Times, 8 January 2004.

59. http://www.economist.com/news/leaders/21599360-government-right-reform-hukou-system-it-needs-be-braver-great

60. *Travels of a T-Shirt in the Global Economy: An Economist Examines the Markets, Power and Politics of World Trade* (Hoboken, NJ: Wiley, 2005).

61. Ibid. p. 99,

62. Ibid. p. 103.

63. "Making Trinkets in China, and a Deadly Dust", *New York Times*, 18 June 2003.

64. "Making Trinkets in China, and a Deadly Dust", *New York Times*, 18 June 2003.

65. "Deceptive Beauty: A Look at the Global Flower Industry" *Global Citizens for a global era;* vol. 1, issue 5. (Victoria, BC: Victoria International Development Education Association, 2002) p. 6.

66. Ibid. p. 7.

67. www.ilo.org/public/english/dialogue/sector/papers/workcolb/1294.htm

68. "Agency Puts Hunger No.1 on List of World's Top Health Risks"" *New York Times*, 31 October 2002.

69. See Fair Trade Update, www.fairtradecertified.org

70. There is some evidence that fair trade is effective in reducing child labor, see Baradaran, Shima and Barclay, Stephanie H., "Fair Trade and Child Labor"*Columbia Human Rights Law Review*, 26 April 2011. Available at SSRN: http://ssrn.com/abstract=1823546

71. See Fair Trade Update, www.fairtradecertified.org

72. "List of tainted peanut butter items in U.S. points to complexity of food production," *New York Times*, 6 February 2009

73. See Ethical Trade Initiative, 11/10/2000 as quoted in William Young and Richard Welford *Ethical Shopping: Where to Shop, What to Buy and What to Do to Make a Difference* (London: Fusion Press, 2002).

74. Medea Benjamin "Wages and Living Expenses for Nike Workers in Indonesia." Global Exchange, Sept. 1998. http://www.globalexchange.org/campaigns/sweatshops/nike/IndonesiaWages.html

75. This study was done by the Marymount University Center for Ethical Concerns. A brief summary of the findings can be found at www.marymount.edu/news/garmetstudy/overview.

76. Daniel W. Elfenbein and Brian McManus, "A Greater Price for a Greater Good? Evidence that Consumers Pay More for Charity-Linked Products" *American Economic Journal: Economic Policy*, vol. 2, no. 2, 2010 pp. 28-60.

77. Behind the Swoosh: Facts about Nike *Citizens for a Global Era* vol. 1, issue 3.

78. For an excellent series on inequality in the United States see Timothy Noah, "The United States of Inequality" in *Slate*: 9/3/2010 http://www.slate.com/id/2266025/entry/2266816/

79. Cited by Barbara Ehrenreich in *Nickel and Dimed: On Not Getting By in America* (Holt: New York, 2007) p. 213.

80. "Walmart Is Said to Be in Talks to Settle Illegal-Immigrant Case," *New York Times*, 5 August 2004.

81. "Walmart Is Said to Be in Talks to Settle Illegal-Immigrant Case," *New York Times*, 5 August 2004.

82. "U.S. Wins Back Pay for Janitors," *New York Times,* 26 August 2004.

83. *Atlanta Journal-Constitution* "Modern-day Slavery Helps Florida's Farms Thrive" 7 December 2003.

84. Barbara Ehrenreich "Wal-Mars Invades Earth" *New York Times* 25 July 2004.

85. http://www.pbs.org/itvs/storewars/stores3.html

Chapter Four

Environmental Justice

"The richest countries of the world, as represented by the G8, have a responsibility to help the poorest. This is not just charity, but a moral obligation. The world's wealthiest countries have emitted more than their fair share of greenhouse gases. Resultant floods, droughts and other climate change impacts continue to fall disproportionately on the world's poorest people and countries, many of which are in Africa." [1]

————Archbishop Desmond Tutu

Up to now I have not asked for much. My proposals really have been too modest! Giving some of one's income to relieve international poverty, advocating for the reform of the rules of international trade and supporting living wage initiatives such as fair trade would not require much of a sacrifice for most of us. Reforming our lives so as to conserve the environment may be more of a challenge. Even the relatively wealthy of the world have become dependent upon lifestyles that are causing global warming and other environmental problems. Starting up our cars, running our air conditioners, and eating meat are directly contributing to global warming and literally endangering millions of people—in the Third World, as well as the first. To change our lifestyles to the point where we would significantly reduce greenhouse gas emissions would require substantial changes in the lives of even the relatively wealthy. [2]

GLOBAL WARMING

A few argue that the scientific arguments that humans are causing global warming are inconclusive, but the vast majority of reputable scientific knowledge takes global warming to be a fact and concludes that human activity is a large factor in the warming. The Intergovernmental Panel on Climate Change (IPCC) is an international group of literally hundreds of respected scientists that was first formed in 1988 by the World Meteorology Association and the United Nations Environmental Program. The IPCC reports should raise alarms. The increase in temperature in the Northern Hemisphere in the twentieth century is the largest increase in the last one thousand years. The report claims that it is very likely that snow coverage has decreased by 10 percent, and, in the Northern Hemisphere, spring and summer sea-ice extent has decreased by about 10–15 percent since the 1950s. Glaciers have decreased in size almost everywhere throughout the world; to take one example, in Switzerland the overall volume of glaciers has decreased by two-thirds.[3] As the world is warming, sea levels are rising. The global average sea level rose between 0.1 and 0.2 meters during the twentieth century. The report gives ample evidence for global warming as well as ample evidence that this warming is the result of human activities.[4] Although the IPCC is perhaps the world's most respected source for information on climate change, it is not the only group documenting the phenomenon. According to a report prepared for the United States Department of Defense, global warming is not only real, but it constitutes one of the greatest challenges to global stability.[5] The Defense Department's report suggested that global warming and the melting of the polar ice caps could alter ocean currents and result in a mini Ice Age in Europe and North America. Failure to prepare for such a scenario could lead to a "significant drop in the human carrying capacity of the Earth's environment."[6]

Rising temperatures are likely to decrease crop yields in many places, in particular in poorer countries that are least well positioned to adapt. According to Worldwatch Institute, plant scientists at the International Rice Research Institute in the Philippines are already noticing damage to crops from rising temperatures in Cambodia, India, and at their own farms. They estimate that, because of global warming, crop yields could drop by 30 percent over the next fifty years, while the region's population is expected to increase by 44 percent.[7] It is not just the heat that will decrease crop yields. Global warming is causing climate to become more erratic. The winter of 2004 was one of the coldest on record, but March 2004 was the third-warmest month ever recorded.[8] In a world where water is at a premium, it makes sense to encourage rice production in areas that are naturally rich in water. But if global warming disrupts natural weather patterns, for example, the monsoons of Asia, then the rice crop that depends upon that water will be impacted as well.

Poor farmers, who farm in marginal areas and rely on nonirrigated farming, are the ones most likely to be most affected by erratic climate. Since 2001 the IPCC has warned that poor countries would be the ones most affected by climate change because the poor do not have the resources to adapt to climate change that the rich have. A report, compiled by fifteen international aid organizations, entitled "Africa—Up in Smoke?" highlights the vulnerability of Africa—the world's poorest continent—to climate change.[9] This report stresses that 70 percent of working people in Africa are employed in small-scale agriculture. These small farms produce most of the food for Africa, and the majority of these farms are dependent on direct rainfall. Given that so many in Africa are poor and directly dependent upon agriculture and given the political instability of the continent and the high rates of disease, it is not surprising that the report continually stresses the vulnerability of the poor in general, and African poor in particular, to climate instability. Wulf Killman, the chairman of the UN Food and Agriculture Organization's climate change group said, "Africa is our greatest worry," "Many countries are already in difficulties . . . and we see a pattern emerging. Southern Africa is definitely becoming drier and everyone agrees that the climate there is changing. We would expect areas that are already prone to drought to become drier with climate change."[10] The UN's famine early warning system director reported that "in southern Africa especially there is no question that drought has become much more frequent in the past few years. There has been a sequence of drought years for four or five years. What is unusual is the repeat patterns."[11]

Climate instability is not the only threat posed to agriculture by global warming. As the seas rise because of global warming, in places such as Thailand, the island nations of the Pacific and Indian Oceans, and the Caribbean Sea, China's Yangtze Delta and Vietnam's Mekong Delta (two of the world's most productive deltas) freshwater is being polluted by rising salt water.[12] Millions of farmers in Egypt living close to the Nile will also be affected. The Nile region is the most densely populated part of Africa and as sea levels rise it will make life difficult for not only those who live in the region, but all Egyptians.[13] In a world where many do not have access to clean drinking water and where farmers need freshwater for crops this is clearly cause for alarm.

As the seas rise because of this warming, many low-lying areas are becoming unsuitable for habitation because of the risk of flooding. As many as 70 million people living in Bangladesh could be affected by the rising seas and an equal number could be affected in China. In 2004, nearly 60 percent of Bangladesh was flooded by monsoons. We don't normally think about the ways that our use of energy threatens to rob those halfway around the world of their land, their drinking water or their food, but the evidence is mounting that this is, in fact, the case. And if concern for others is not enough to make us stop polluting, then perhaps concern for our own safety will. As a United States Defense Department study underlines, threats to the stability of large numbers of people across the globe is very likely to be a threat to the stability of wealthy nations as well.

Groups large and small are being affected. One Inuit village in Alaska, Shishmaref, has lost more than 90 meters of coastline in the past thirty years—half of it since 1997. It has been estimated that it will cost $100 million to move the residents to more stable ground.[14] The Inuit people sought a ruling from the Inter-American Commission on Human Rights stating that the United States is threatening their way of life by its contributions to global warming.[15] Given that climate changes are affecting their way of life, the Inuit are claiming that global warming is a human rights issue. Although the commission has no enforcement power, a ruling against the United States would have opened the way for lawsuits against the United States or against companies from the United States. The lawsuit was supported by a study by more than three hundred scientists from eight countries with Arctic territory and concluded that "human influences" are the dominant factor in the changing climatic conditions in the Arctic. The United States, along with 180 other nations, has signed the United Nations Framework Convention on Climate Change. The Framework Convention called for greenhouse gases to be stabilized at safe levels. The developed nations also committed themselves to return to the 1990 level of emissions by 2000, although this provision was not legally binding and, in fact, the nations did not come close to meeting that goal.[16] The representatives of the Inuit met with the United Nations Ambassador from Tuvalu, an island halfway between Hawaii and Australia that is being threatened by rising oceans. The Inter-American Commission on Human Rights rejected the petition without prejudice in 2006, claiming that it was unable to determine whether the alleged facts would "tend to characterize a violation of rights protected by the American Declaration." Still, as the evidence for the effects of climate change becomes more established, we can expect more lawsuits to be filed. If indeed, as there is good reason to suspect, the Inuit's lifestyle is being affected by greenhouse emissions, then there clearly is both an ethical and a legal obligation to make amends.

As "Africa—Up in Smoke?" emphasizes, the countries and the people least responsible for global warming stand to be the ones most affected. The report estimates that there are probably more environmental refugees today than there are political refugees. Not all environmental refugees are fleeing manmade disasters, but the number affected by climate change is estimated to rise dramatically as the planet heats up. The World Health Organization estimates that 160,000 people die each year due to climate change.[17] The poor are, in this case as in many others, unacknowledged and unappreciated benefactors to the wealthy. The poor pay for the pollution that the wealthy produce. If the poor were using energy at the rate that the rich use it, not only would energy be being depleted at a much more rapid rate, but the problem of global warming would be even more difficult to solve. Anil Agarwal and Sunita Narain use the metaphor of the global sink to illustrate the problem.[18]

In 1990, India had 16.2 percent of the world's population, but contributed just 6 percent of the carbon dioxide and 14.4 percent of the methane to the world's atmosphere. The United States, however, had only 4.73 percent of the world's population, but contributed 26 percent of the carbon dioxide and 20 percent of the methane. Today China is the world's leader in greenhouse gas emissions and India is producing much more than it did when Agarwal and Narain wrote their article. The world has a limited ability to absorb greenhouse gases. The wealthy are using more than their share of the greenhouse gas sink. The obvious conclusion is that the wealthy should pay the poor because of their overuse of the global sink. In 1991, the United States would have owed $6.3 billion for its overuse of the sink. India would have been owed $8.3 billion. Since 1991, when Agarwal and Narain's article was written, greenhouse gas emissions have continued to rise. As China and India industrialize, the problem is getting worse. Between 1990 and 2003, U.S. energy-related carbon emissions rose by 16 percent. China's emissions have gone up about 47 percent since 1990. China currently contributes about 29 percent of the world's carbon emissions and as it continues to develop this will go higher. Of course much of the emissions are coming from the industries that are making exports being sold to people all over the world.

Thanks to economic development, more and more of the world's citizens want the basic necessities, such as comfortable homes and refrigeration. A World Bank study reported that transportation is the fastest-growing consumer of fossil fuels and the fastest-growing source of CO2 emissions.[19] More people in the developing world are able to buy conveniences, such as private automobiles, that many in the United States have come to expect. In 1990, there were by one estimate 560 million automobiles in the world—175 million in the United States alone. China had 6 million cars in 2000, up from 1.1 million in 1990, and India had 6.1 million cars in 2000, up from 1.7 in 1990. In 2006, there were 20 million passenger cars on the road in China and car sales were up by 54 percent during the first three months of 2006.[20] In 2011 there were, according to one estimate, more than 90 million motor vehicles on the roads in China and it had become the largest market for motor vehicles in the world.[21] By 2050, according to one projection, India will have the largest number of cars of any country, 611 million.[22] The Chinese have recognized these problems and are making a major effort to develop electric vehicles. It would be easy for the United States to pay $6.3 billion. Reducing world emissions will not be easy, particularly as many people the world over begin to live as people in wealthy nations live now. How can we tell the rest of the world not to pollute as we have done and still do?

At times, it has been argued that the United States, and other wealthy nations, should have the right to pollute more given that they produce more, but that argument seems weak. We should aggregate consumption given that much of what the United States produces, and, as I have already said, indeed much of what China, India and the rest of the Third World produces, the wealthy consume. To put the point more concretely, none of us have the right to consume so much that we endanger the poor living in low-lying areas of Bangladesh or contribute to the salinization of the Mekong Delta and the Nile.

Agarwal and Narain's argument would be stronger if it recognized the differences within nations. There are within the United States, for example, some who live without automobiles and air conditioning. Within the Third World, there are a more and more people who drive gas-guzzling cars and have plenty of air conditioning. National statistics give us an idea of the scope of the problem, but given the vast differences between individual carbon footprints, questions of ethical responsibility and justice require that each individual examine his or her contribution to global warming.[23] One study frames the issue this way. If we used fossil fuels more efficiently and made greater use of renewable resources, the world could provide everyone with modest but comfortable homes, refrigeration for food—a necessity given that food-borne diseases are rampant without refrigeration—access to public transportation and occasional use of a car.[24] The world simply cannot support everyone living the way that many of us currently live. We all need to do energy audits. As I have already said, some people living in wealthy nations, particularly some living in the United States, do not have air conditioning and do not have personal vehicles. More and more people in emerging countries—remember the 611 million automobiles that Indians will own by 2050—are gaining access to a life that relies on extensive use of fossil fuels. It is truly frightening to think about how endangered our planet is from the new consumers of the emerging countries. It is also very hard to tell them to reduce their carbon footprint if we do nothing about our own profligate lifestyles. As the world develops, our environment cannot continue to support our current lifestyle. Those of us who drive gas-burning cars and have access to air conditioning and central heating—whether we live in a wealthy nation or a poor nation—are contributing more than our fair share to the global sink and we are using more than our share of nonrenewable resources. All of us who are using more than our fair share of the global sink right now owe a debt to those who are not driving cars and not using air conditioning. Thanks to their abstinence, our world has a chance to overcome the threat of global warming. But we really are all in this together, or as Richard Miller puts it, we are all on the same team when it comes to climate control.[25]

It is true that many of us looking to cut back on our emissions are constrained by factors that are very difficult to control—such as our access to public transportation or whether our power is supplied by dirty coal burning power plants or clean renewable energy, but perhaps we have more power than we think. Ursula Sladek was a homemaker and mother of four children when the Chernobyl accident deposited radioactive fallout in her small town of Schoenau in Germany's Black Forest. As a result, she helped to form a power company that provides power to her local power grid from renewable sources. The company stresses energy efficiency and provides incentives to its customers to reduce their usage of energy. The company generates 30 percent of the power the town needs locally using small hydroelectric projects, solar panels, windmills and twenty small machines, placed in people's homes, about the size of washing machines, that produce heat for a home and power for the grid. The company gets the rest of the renewable power by buying from other renewable sources. A reform in Germany now allows her company to sell its renewable power all over Germany and the company currently has 110,000 customers who pay the same rate as the customers who buy from companies whose power comes from nonrenewable sources. The company aims to have a million customers by 2015. There is a similar movement to create a renewable power company in Marin County in California as well.[26] In important ways the German government has come around to Sladek's way of thinking. It aims to have Germany produce all of its power from renewable sources by 2050.

Even if we do not start our own renewable energy company, we should be lobbying our government to support energy conservation and development of more renewable sources of energy. Wind power has great potential in many parts of the world. China is investing a great deal in it. Google, renowned for its business acumen and farsightedness, is investing $5 billion in transmission lines that would conduct 7,000 megawatts of electricity from offshore windmills to the eastern coast of the United States. Wind power is relatively inexpensive, and the industry's rapid growth is a testament to the market's current faith in wind power's economic viability. In the United States it has been estimated that wind power could account for 20 percent of the nation's energy supply by 2030.[27]

Solar power is another renewable energy source that should be encouraged. Currently solar power provides less than 1 percent of the world's electricity output, but it is also the world's fastest-growing energy source. Japan has set as a goal to generate 10 percent of its electricity needs through solar power by 2030.[28] Solar power is conveniently available at some of the times when power is needed most, for example, when the sun is shining is also the time when people in hot climates, who can afford it, use air conditioning. It can often be used in conjunction with wind power. Environmentally friendly energy production and conservation will not only cut down on global warming, but will also leave the air we breathe cleaner. It will also make oil importers like the United States less vulnerable to interruptions in oil supplies as well as undercut repressive regimes that rely on mineral wealth to hold on to power. The development of these industries can be an important source of new jobs. Moreover, we should be making the change to renewable now. The longer we wait to address the problem of greenhouse gases the more expensive it will be to fix.

For many of us, it would not be easy to cut back on our driving. In the United States, most of our cities and suburbs have done little to encourage mass transit or bicycles. Many of us do, however, often have the option to buy fuel-efficient automobiles as well as to seek out opportunities to carpool. Those living in cold climates are going to need energy for heat and those living in hot climates will need energy for cooling. All of us, however, should think hard about the energy efficiency of our residences. Large, inefficient residences require enormous amounts of energy, and the world simply cannot support the wide-scale adoption of such patterns of consumption. There is a principle that is often discussed in beginning economics textbooks that the producer should pay for the full costs of production. If, for example, a factory produces something, but saves money by releasing polluted water into a river, then everyone downstream is paying for the factory's failure to clean the water.

Many places in the United States have made it particularly difficult to live without owning an automobile. People the world over should lobby our governments to plan development in such a way that people are able to walk, ride bicycles and use public transportation. Communities that decrease our reliance on automobiles and encourage us to walk and ride bicycles will not only bring ecological benefits, but they will also encourage healthy lifestyles. In 1960, the average American drove about 4,000 miles a year. In 2000, the average number of miles driven each year was nearly 10,000.[29] The time spent stuck in traffic has dramatically increased in almost all major metropolitan areas in the United States. For example, in 1960, in Atlanta a driver could expect to spend six hours stuck in traffic each year. In 2002, they spent thirty-four hours in traffic.[30] Given the way that many of our communities are built—often lacking even sidewalks, not to mention stores and points of interest within walking distance—it is little wonder that the number of overweight Americans has grown from 24 percent in 1960 to 64 percent in 2000. Being overweight increases one's risk of cancer, heart disease, stroke, high blood pressure, and arthritis, among other diseases.[31] Asthma is another disease that is linked to air quality. In short, the wealthy's reliance on the automobile, in particular, and our inefficient use of energy, in general, is neither healthy nor pleasant (especially when one is stuck in traffic), nor good for the poor, who are most susceptible to the effects of global warming. It is also not good for the poor in the United States. Lack of convenient and inexpensive public transportation makes life difficult for those who cannot afford an automobile as well as for the elderly and others who cannot drive.

Urban design in the United States has very measurable effects on people of color and the poor of all races living within our borders. Minorities are disproportionately exposed to polluted air, in particular, and, in general, they are more likely to suffer the effects of urban planning centered around the "needs" of the rich.[32] The rate of asthma among AfricanAmericans is 22 percent higher than the rate among white Americans, and the rate of mortality from asthma is three times higher in blacks than whites.[33] Black children are 64 percent more likely than white children to have asthma. Other minorities in the United States suffer as well. Black children are 93 percent more likely to be hospitalized for asthma than white children and Latino children are 34 percent more likely to be hospitalized for asthma than whites. One study done in Atlanta reported that pedestrian fatality rates between 1994–1998 were 9.74 per 100,000 for Hispanics, 3.85 for blacks and 1.64 for whites. Poor urban planning is not only contributing to poor air quality, it is literally killing pedestrians—many of whom are simply too poor to own private vehicles. We cannot change urban planning overnight, but to the extent that we can change our communities in order to reduce our energy consumption, we may very well find that we live happier, healthier lives while at the same time reducing the rate of global warming. Working to reduce global warming could also help us rectify the disproportionate burden of poverty shouldered by the poor living in the United States. There is little point in asking people to make large sacrifices, such as giving up their cars, that will significantly impair their ability to earn a living, but asking people to drive fuel-efficient cars does not seem like much of a sacrifice. Similarly giving up air conditioning or heating can be very onerous and even life-threatening, but asking people to be more frugal in their use of energy seems like a very modest request given how serious the effects of global warming are and will be on many of the world's poorest people. Finally, it seems unproblematic to say that if we are contributing to the problem, because it would be very difficult for us to live without contributing to the problem, then we ought to work so that cohabitation on our planet becomes something other than the right of the powerful to live in such a way that the most vulnerable are at risk.

THE PRODUCTION OF MEAT

In the United States there are many of us who would like to take public transportation but do not have that option, and there might be many more who would find that they would use and enjoy public transportation if they had efficient public transportation options. Most of us do, however, have control over our diets. Some have argued that we can have an important effect on our carbon footprint by buying locally grown products, but others have pointed out that local is not always better in terms of carbon footprint. For example, Peter Singer and Jim Mason argue that if a local farmer uses a heater to keep his or her greenhouse warm then she or he is probably using more fuel per pound of tomatoes than it would cost to grow the tomato in a warmer climate and ship it to the colder climate. They based their conclusions on quick calculations that they made after talking to a local farmer who used a heater merely to supplement solar power in his greenhouse. Singer and Mason also cite a British study that concluded tomatoes grown in Britain outside of the normal growing season emit three times the carbon dioxide as tomatoes grown in Spain and then trucked to Britain. In addition, they cite a Swedish study which showed that buying locally grown carrots did save energy because the carrots were grown without artificial heat. It was more efficient in terms of energy use to grow tomatoes in Spain and truck them to Britain.[34] Local is not always better, at least not from an environmental standpoint. If one country's food production processes are not efficient and transportation is, it may make more environmental sense to produce the product in the more efficient country and ship it to the less efficient country. It may also be the case that those farmers who live farther away are poorer and have less of a social net to fall back on.

On the other hand, many have argued that we can make a difference in our carbon footprint if we switch from eating meat, in particular if we switch from eating beef, to a plant-based diet. The consumption of meat is a luxury which, for the most part, only the relatively wealthy can afford in any great quantity. There is a raging debate in the United States about how much the production of meat contributes to greenhouse gas emissions and about the efficiency of the meat industry. The production of meat contributes to global warming. The meat industry produces three greenhouse gases: carbon dioxide (CO_2), methane (CH_4) and nitrogen (N_2O). There are direct and indirect ways that the raising of animals contributes to global warming. Cows produce large amounts of methane gases—20 percent of methane gas that is released into the atmosphere every year come from cows. Methane is a potent greenhouse gas; "it traps twenty-five times as much heat from the sun as carbon dioxide."[35] According to EPA estimates, ruminant livestock accounts for 28 percent of global methane emissions from human-related activities.[36] Methane is also increasing in our atmosphere at a faster rate than carbon dioxide. Nitrogen is an even more potent greenhouse gas than methane. It is 310 times more potent than CO_2 and the primary source of this gas is fertilizer used in agriculture.[37] This gas is also released when animal manure and urine is spread on soil. The production of meat leads to global warming in other ways as well. In the United States and other places, the crops that are grown and then fed to animals are grown with fertilizers that produce greenhouse gases. The storage of animal waste in lagoons gives off greenhouse gases and, particularly in the developing world, there is a large amount of land that is being cleared to raise animals. This land clearing is, most scientists believe, the industry's largest single contributor to greenhouse gas emissions.

In 2006, the United Nations Food and Agricultural Organization released a report with the startling claim that globally the livestock sector was responsible for more greenhouse gas emissions than the transportation sector.[38] This news was conveyed to the general public with articles such as "Meat, the Gas Guzzler" that was published in the *New York Times* in January 2008. Some researchers questioned the FAO's claim. Most prominently, Frank Mitloehner argued that the FAO's claim was flawed because it compared the amount of greenhouse gases generated throughout the entire life cycle of meat, from the clearing of land to placing a package of meat on the grocery store shelf to the amount of greenhouse gases produced by the burning of fuels in vehicles. The FAO did not include in the comparison, for example, how much greenhouse gas is produced in the manufacturing of vehicles or in the drilling and refining of oil. In addition, Mitloehner argues that meat and more intensive farming methods, particularly in the developing world, could be beneficial for both the global poor and the environment. He argues, as do others, that cows fed on grain live shorter lives and therefore emit less methane.[39] He also argues that growing grain and then feeding it to a cow takes up less land than allowing a cow to graze on grasslands.[40] Less land for cows could mean more land for carbon-absorbing forests, although others point out that cow pastures also absorb greenhouse gases. Mitloehner maintains that meat raised in the United States creates a much smaller amount of greenhouse gases than the FOA report suggested. He calculates that the raising of animals creates about 3 percent of greenhouse gases produced in the United States. This seems in line with the United States Environmental Protection Agency's claim that all agriculture contributes about 6 percent of greenhouse gas emissions.[41] The proponents of the industry argue that meat, properly raised, is a very efficient source of protein.

Mitloehner seems to agree (he cites without objecting) with the FAO report that deforestation in Latin America is "the primary source for greenhouse gas emissions associated with global livestock production." In the United States we are actually increasing the amount of forest lands, but Brazil and Indonesia, in particular, are turning forests into grazing lands. The resulting destruction of these forests is releasing a great deal of greenhouse gases. Seventy percent of Brazil's CO2 emissions come from deforestation.[42] According to some reports, the rate of deforestation in Brazil has dropped by two-thirds since 2000. Brazil has committed to reducing greenhouse emissions by 39 percent by 2020 and it claims to be on track to do this.[43] Indonesia and Brazil are doing what the United States has already done—changing their land to promote development. In Brazil, much of the newly deforested land is used to grow soybeans which are then often exported to Europe to serve as feed for cows. In Indonesia the cleared land is often used to grow palm trees to produce palm oil for biofuels. It is hard to tell these countries not to do what the United States has already done, particularly in light of greater needs of the people of these countries. Brazil has recognized the problems that the clearing of forests pose and is acting to curb it. Even though the United States is currently adding more forest than it cuts down, we are benefiting from the clearing that took place in the past. Granted, that clearing was done, for the most part, at a time when we had no idea of the coming problem of greenhouse gases. Still, the current U.S. meat industry is only possible given the massive amount of land that has been cleared. If instead of producing crops for the meat industry, more land was replanted with forests, these forests could help reabsorb the carbon that was released when the forests were cut down. The world needs to stop removing forests, but it seems patently unfair to ask the rural poor of Brazil and Indonesia (to mention only two of the largest countries involved) to shoulder the burden without compensation.

Environmental problems like this show how interconnected the world is today. We all have an interest in slowing or even reversing the destruction of rainforests. Well, not exactly. The Brazilian farmer is trying to make a living while the native resident of the rain forest is trying to preserve her or his way of life. Poor farmers the world over who rely on regular rains have an interest in lower carbon emissions as do the residents of low-lying areas in places such as Bangladesh and Florida. Why should the farmers, the poor or even the middle class in Brazil and Indonesia—to name only some of the biggest players—forgo the benefits that the conversion of the land to crop-lands can bring? One could argue that many—but not all!—in the United States have enjoyed the benefits of the rapid rise in carbon emissions—fuel in our cars, air conditioning and heating, not to mention a mind numbing number of consumer products while billions have been left out. The skies should belong to all of us, but some of us have been leading lives that have flooded them with gases that are beginning to harm all of us. The poor are usually the first to be harmed. Each of us, or at least everyone one of us who has access to the internet needs to do a greenhouse gas audit of our lives and figure out how we can cut back on our emissions.

Even if Mitloehner is right that the United States' agricultural industry is not as big a contributor to the greenhouse gas problem as many have thought how efficient is it to grow plants and then feed them to animals? Is the way we currently raise meat sustainable or are we using up nonrenewable re-sources for short-term gains? Traditionally, animals were raised on land un-suitable for farming. This is usually a productive use of the land if the land is suitable for grazing. In the United States, we feed a great deal of grain to cows, chickens and pigs that are raised for meat. Many argue that this is wasteful, particularly in the case of cows, for many reasons. First, it is argued that this is not energy efficient. It is difficult to calculate exactly how much protein we feed cows and exactly how much we get out. Typically cows in the United States are born in a pasture and then sent to a feedlot and fed corn, not because corn is best suited to them, but because it has been a highly subsidized crop. Hence humans in the United States consume vast amounts of high-fructose corn syrup and cows and other animals (even farm-raised salmon!) consume vast amounts of corn. But feedlots do not only feed them corn, they also often give the cows by-products from other industries. It has been reported that in Nebraska the makers of ethanol and corn syrup feed their by-products to animals and it would be "devastating" to these industries if they had to dispose of these products in landfills. In California, rice hulls, almond hulls and citrus pulp are among the "waste products" that are fed to animals.[44] Feeding these things to the cows not only reduces the amount of grains the animals consume, it also saves some greenhouse gas emissions that would have arisen from disposing of these things in landfills. Cows can also be fed blood, pork protein, horse protein, chicken protein, fish protein, and recovered waste products from humans' plates.

Only about 600 pounds of a beef cow are actually edible, and some of those 600 pounds are things such as liver and intestines, which are edible, but are not often eaten in the United States. If you consider only the red meat it may be closer to the truth to say that it takes almost 20 pounds of corn to produce 1 pound of red meat.[45] Other animals, such as pigs and chickens, are more efficient in converting plants to protein. The meat industry points out that when calculating the environmental costs of livestock production we must not forget that other parts of the animal are used as well. Without leather from cowhides, we would probably have to use more plastics and there are obviously environmental costs, including the production of greenhouse gases, that are associated with plastics.

Can the earth produce enough grain to supply the wealthy's desire for meat and still feed the poor? Amartya Sen argues that there is no world food crisis and that food production by head has been steadily growing everywhere except Africa.[46] Proponents of the U.S. meat industry claim that it is efficient and could be a model for the world. It is difficult to say exactly how efficient the production of meat is, and the problems are compounded even more when we try to judge the ethics of eating any particular piece of meat. Worldwatch Institute concluded that "American feed (for livestock) takes so much energy to grow that it might as well be a petroleum byproduct."[47] The Union of Concerned Scientists concluded that driving cars that get poor gas mileage and eating beef are the two most damaging things that residents of the United States do that contributes to global warming.[48] But if the production of meat only contributes 3 percent of U.S. greenhouse gases, is this true? On the other hand, it is one thing to say the United States' meat industry only contributes 3 percent of greenhouse gases, but if meat eaters in the United States are eating meat from cows raised in recently cleared pastures in other countries, then the amount of greenhouse gases attributed to *consumers* living in the United States goes up considerably. Similarly, if Brazilian soy is going to feed European cattle, then European meat eaters are contributing to the problem of deforestation and hence greenhouse gases.

One study concluded that changing from a meat to a vegan diet (and this would mean giving up dairy products as well) would save as much energy as switching from a car that got 24 miles to the gallon to a car that gets 51 miles to the gallon. The paper concluded that if the entire nation switched to a plant-based diet it would reduce by 6 percent the United States' greenhouse gas emissions. Another study reported that it takes 6 to 17 times as much land to produce a unit of protein from meat as it does from soy.[49] A third study focused on beef and dairy and calculated that eating only locally grown food is not nearly as effective in combating global warming as giving up red meat and dairy products.[50] I am not suggesting that anyone do any of these things. I am certainly not suggesting that the government force dramatic changes in our lives by implementing radical draconian reforms such as banning meat. It is much easier to see the problems than figure out the answers. But information is needed to determine where we should place our efforts. At the very least we can see that red meat and dairy are major contributors to greenhouse gases and we might think about moderating our intake of these products. And the government might think about taking steps so that we are indeed paying the full price of our consumption. I can't imagine a good argument for the current corn subsidies!

Lurking behind many of these discussions are questions about the agricultural techniques. Some say that without intensive use of fertilizer and industrialized farming we will never be able to feed the world. On the other side you have people who claim that modern farming techniques often produce short-term gains by using unsustainable practices that lead, for example, to soil erosion and water depletion. Many think there is something to be said for both of these views. Many new techniques have been employed in the last few years, such as no-till planting, that have reduced the greenhouse gas emissions of agriculture. Those who say that high-intensity meat production in the United States is actually an efficient industry also draw comparisons to other agricultural practices. For example, the cultivation of rice produces large amounts of greenhouse gases. In fact it produces large amounts of the very same gas that the cows produce, methane. Unlike beef, which is reserved for a wealthy few, the cultivation of rice may be the most important economic activity on earth. Nearly half of the world's people eat rice at least once a day. In many places there has been a concerted effort to improve crop yields through, among other things, nitrogen fertilizer. The use of this fertilizer also contributes to global warming. The amount of methane produced by the cultivation of rice depends a great deal on how the crop is managed, and there are efforts to reduce the amount of methane the crop produces, but no matter how rice is grown it is going to emit greenhouse gases. According to Darren Hudson, one acre of rice gives off the same amount of methane in a year as a feedlot of fifty-five thousand cows. It is difficult to know exactly how he calculates this given that, among other things, he does not seem to take into account that the greenhouse gases produced in rice production vary widely. It is also not clear if he is counting the greenhouse gases that went into the growing of the grain that the cows eat. Hudson also points out that those cows provide much more protein than the rice and rice production uses a great deal of water.[51] If we ask meat lovers to give up their steak, are we going to ask half the world to give up their daily bowl of rice?

Such is the stuff that philosophers' dreams, and everyone else's nightmares, are made of. These goals are worthy of crusades or Plato's ideal city, but they demand a dislocation of people's lives that is unwise and unrealistic. It is warranted, wise, and realistic to live our lives in more responsible ways so that we are conserving our environment, and protecting the vulnerable. We need smart government policies that move people and industries in the right direction without massive dislocation as well as individual acts that address these issues without causing huge amounts of harm. The phasing out of ozone-depleting gases, that was done with very little large-scale disruption, and not the Great Leap Forward should be our model.

Greenhouse gases are not the only problem associated with the production of meat. We are also using large amounts of water in the production of grain that we then feed to animals.[52] Almost half of the water used annually in the United States goes to produce feed and provide drinking water for livestock. Much of this water comes from underground reservoirs, many of which took a very long time to form, but are now being used up at alarming rates. The Ogallala Aquifer is believed to be one of the largest bodies of fresh water on earth. David Brauer of the U.S. Agricultural Service reports that in "a short half century we have drawn the Ogallala level down from an average of 240 feet to about 80."[53] Brauer claims that the water is going to run out in the near future, but he hopes that improved conservation can make the water last for another eighty years. Farmers have adapted by improving their irrigation and tilling methods, and planting crops that require less water, but Brauer believes that all we can do at this point is to prepare for the aquifer's demise. What nature took millions of years to collect we will use up in a century.

As the rest of the world begins to eat more meat, water is being used up at alarming rates. India, China, North Africa, and the United States are all depleting their aquifers.[54] To the extent that we are using water at an unsustainable rate to produce crops to feed to animals, we are merely putting off the day of reckoning when grain production will fall. Louis XV, who is said to have spent his time cavorting while France went to seed, is infamously purported to have said, "After me, the deluge." Those of us who are participating in the using of aquifers should have the honesty to say, if we don't change our lifestyles and lobby our governments to protect this precious source, "After us, the drought."

In addition to using up water, there may also be a problem of using up soil. This is an issue which received a great deal of attention in the 90s in the United States and claims were made that it had been addressed. A recent article, however, argued that Iowa was losing far more topsoil than had been previously estimated.[55] If we are using up large aquifers and soil, those costs need to be considered when doing the efficiency equation. As Paul Krugman notes, it is an almost universally accepted economic principle that people should pay the true social cost of their actions.[56] Quoting from a standard economics textbook, Krugman makes the point that the great majority of economists believe that government must intervene in the marketplace to insure that polluters or those who use up natural resources, such as water or the carbon sink, pay. With the aquifers the modus operandi seems to be use it up before anyone notices and then, those who can, get out of town.

Another challenge that meat poses is what to do with animal excrement. Organic waste from livestock is, along with pesticides, chemical fertilizers, agricultural salts and sediments, the primary nonpoint source of water pollution in the United States. At times, there are dramatic spills. On June 21, 1995, a seven-and-one-half-acre lagoon holding 25 million gallons of hog urine and feces spilled into the New River in North Carolina. By contrast the *ExxonValdez* spilled "only" 12 million gallons of oil. We are much more aware of the Exxon spill, but how many have heard of the New River spill? It has been estimated that the concentration of pathogens in hog waste is 10–100 times greater than the concentration in human waste. Chicken waste is also a problem. According to the government's General Accounting Office, in 1995, there were about two thousand poultry operations that were so large that they were required to obtain a discharge permit under the Clean Water Act, but only thirty-nine had, in fact, done so.[57]

Many studies have documented pollution from factory farms. For example, the Centers for Disease Control and Prevention suggests that there could be a link between spontaneous abortions in humans and the high nitrate levels in Indiana well water found close to feedlots.[58] Another study in North Carolina found severe seepage losses of nitrogen from more than 50 percent of the lagoons tested by the state.[59] As the previously mentioned study from Indiana showed, elevated nitrates in groundwater poses serious health risks. Most of those who are directly affected are the poor and often nonwhite people living close to these factory farms. One study investigated the health and quality of life of residents living near hog farms, and cattle farms and compared these two groups to a control group.[60] Those living close to the six thousand head hog operation and the intensive cattle farms "reported increased occurrences of headaches, runny nose, sore throat, excessive coughing, diarrhea, and burning eyes." In addition, those living close to the hogs reported that they often could not open their windows or even go outside even when the weather was nice. The majority of people surveyed were African-Americans, which should not surprise us given that 2,500 intensive hog operations in North Carolina tend to be located in areas that are poor and nonwhite. In short, factory farming disproportionately affects the poor, both at home and abroad. Those who eat meat rarely think about the runny noses, sore throats, burning eyes and bouts of diarrhea suffered by those who live next to the factory farms. The poor, both at home and abroad, who take much of the burden of our environmentally wasteful ways are, for the most part, out of sight and out of mind. In many ways the poor living next to large meat operations are like canaries in the mine or the recipients of subprime mortgages in the United States. They are some of the most vulnerable and represent a warning that the current practices are dangerous. If left unchecked, these practices are very likely to harm many more of us.

We should also consider whether our love of meat outweighs our need for effective antibiotics. Seventy percent of all antimicrobial drugs produced in the United States are fed to cows, pigs and chickens.[61] Such widespread usage of these drugs degrades their effectiveness and threatens to encourage the development of superbugs. Although we all stand to suffer from this it is not hard to imagine that the poor probably have the most to lose. The poor will be the ones who are less likely to have access to the costlier new antibiotics. To support our cheap meat habit, we are sacrificing the effectiveness of drugs.

There are numerous indications that diets with less meat are healthier, and there are also many questions about the unnecessary infliction of pain on animals. I take both of these concerns seriously, but here I want to raise questions about the contributions that the meat industry makes to the problem of global warming and if its inefficiencies pose a threat to good stewardship of the earth's precious resources. Even an efficiently raised cow—just as an efficient rice paddy—contributes to rising sea levels, contamination of drinking water, and unstable climate conditions! All of us, meat eaters or vegetarians should think about our patterns of consumption. We should raise questions that push rice growers and the meat industry to be more efficient and better stewards. We should support measures that lower our carbon footprint as well as measures designed to promote sustainable agriculture. I certainly would not begrudge poor people the protein that cheap factory farms provide, nor poor rice eaters their bowl of rice from an inefficient paddy. I have a great deal more sympathy for poor farmers—growing rice or raising beef—and realize that they will need help to reduce their greenhouse gas emissions. If we are lucky enough not to be one of the billions who are scrounging a daily meal, we need to think about the patterns of our consumption and play constructive roles in managing the world's precious resources. We should lobby for research that will improve agricultural efficiency and promote good stewardship. The United States is a very wealthy country with a large number of very poor people. The United States controls some of the world's most fertile farmlands. As an article from the *Telegraph* points out, the depletion of the Ogallala Aquifer is not just a problem for Texas' farmers. Irrigated plains grow 20 percent of U.S. grains ,and, without that cheap food, world food markets would be considerably tighter. Many of the world's poor directly or indirectly depend on cheap U.S. food. The *world* cannot afford to lose these valuable agricultural lands. To the extent that we use up water and soil for short-term gains we are depriving not just the future generations of this country, but the future generations of the world, of food. We can quickly use up the water, the soil and the world's greenhouse gas sink living lives of relative luxury on our humble Versailles or we can examine our lives and our government's policies and try to protect and preserve the world's air, earth and water for future generations.

OUR WASTE

Montaigne wrote in his essay "Of Vanity" that he knew of a man who used "the working of his belly" to impart to others knowledge of his life. The unnamed man had on display in his house seven or eight chamber pots so that his guests could see what his belly had produced during the week. These chamber pots were his object of study and his chief conversation topic. Montaigne writes that all other subjects of conversation "stank in his nostrils."[62] By looking at the things we discard and thinking about where these things end up, it might give us a new appreciation for the true cost of our lifestyles.

The range of hazardous wastes produced to support even middle-class lives is vast. They may be the by-product of, industry, hospitals, pharmaceuticals products, wood-preserving chemicals, mineral waste oils and emulsions, inks, dyes, paints, lacquers, refineries, and transport services. In other words, hazardous waste is our spent batteries, our paint thinner, the oil from our cars, the nuclear fuel used to generate our power and the needles used to draw our blood. Hazardous wastes may be hazardous in many ways. They can be explosive, flammable, poisonous, infectious, corrosive or toxic.[63] There are two main categories of hazardous waste disposal. At times, wastes are recycled, recovered, and in some cases, even reused. At other times, hazardous wastes are stored in what is supposed to be a "final resting place." Even in the United States, there are questions about how final such resting places are. It has been reported, for example, that in the United States there is considerable leakage from waste storage units into groundwater.

It has been estimated that 95 percent of hazardous waste shipped from the First World to the Third World is supposedly destined to be recycled.[64] But there are numerous reports of sham recycling schemes, and, even when recycling does take place, it has been reported that the recycling takes place under extremely hazardous conditions. Greenpeace reported on the unsafe way in which small shops in the Philippines recycled batteries. There is also a famous case of a mercury recycling center in South Africa that was found to be unsafe. The plant, run by the British company Thor Chemicals, imported thousands of tons of waste from the United States and Europe between 1986 and 1994. Tests showed high levels of mercury contamination around the plant. Two workers at the plant died of mercury poisoning and almost 30 percent were shown to be at risk of severe mercury poisoning. India, China and Bangladesh are home to facilities that take apart old ships. Old ships are not officially labeled hazardous waste, but the workers are exposed to toxic chemicals, and it has been estimated that 25 percent of the workers who labor in this industry will come down with cancer from the asbestos on these ships.[65]

In 1995, the United States exported less than 1 percent of its hazardous wastes and most of those went to Canada.[66] Even if they are exported, there can be good reasons to do so. Industrialized countries sometimes take wastes from other industrialized countries because the source that has generated the waste is close to the facility that can process or store the waste. Only a small percentage of the hazardous wastes from industrialized nations end up in the poor nations of the Third World, but some do. Toxic wastes from the United States have been dumped in Brazil, Haiti, Nigeria, South Africa and Zimbabwe. It is often hard for poor countries to say no. For example, Guinea-Bissau entered into an agreement to take hazardous waste from Britain and Switzerland in exchange for $600 million. That offer was hard to refuse given that this was more than four times greater than Guinea-Bissau's GNP.[67] Fortunately, the deal never went through because of public pressure in the African nation.

In 1989, a convention was negotiated called the Basel Agreement, which does not ban the exportation of hazardous waste, but requires that countries be informed when hazardous wastes are being shipped through, or into, their territory. Most developing nations wanted a ban on exporting hazardous wastes, but the wealthy industrialized nations fought hard against such a ban. There are arguments to be made against a blanket ban. India, for example, like many foreign countries, needs lead for its car batteries and relies on recycling lead from old batteries for much of its lead needs. Banning the importation of old batteries would put many small businesses out of business, but the current practices may very well be killing many workers. There are some arguments in favor of a ban against the exportation of hazardous wastes. One could argue that wealthy nations should be responsible for cleaning up the hazardous waste that their industries have produced. For that matter, we could argue that wealthy communities within the United States should not dump their hazardous wastes in the backyards of the poor within their own borders. Society's hazardous wastes often end up in the backyard of the poor. In the United States, hazardous waste incinerators are often found in poor neighborhoods and we have already seen that large pools of animal waste are found in rural areas.

Zada Lipman argues that Third World countries should receive aid so that they do not need to rely on recycling or storing hazardous wastes. They should also receive assistance so that they can safely dispose of the hazardous wastes that they themselves generate and develop cleaner industries that generate fewer hazardous wastes. Some groups doubt whether hazardous waste recycling can ever be done properly in the third world. The Basel Action Network argues that old televisions and computers that are sent to China, India and Nigeria for recycling often end up being merely smashed and burned. It argues that it is only in the United States that we can be sure that hazardous wastes "are recycled in a clean, green and fully transparent manner."[68] I do not doubt that it is often the case that recycling of hazardous waste is not done properly in the global south. For that matter, it is often not done properly in the United States. There are televisions, computers and cell phones all over the world that need to be recycled. Instead of insisting on doing all recycling here, perhaps we should work to develop proper recycling across the world. As flat-screen TVs, computers, and other electronics proliferate around the world, there is a need for these recycling centers around the world as well.

We may not think of ourselves as producers of hazardous waste, or as squanderers of top soil, wasters of water, or producers of greenhouse gases, but chances are that we contribute to all of these problems. I can barely remember how many computers and cell phones I have gone through. Montaigne's friend spent his days pondering the waste that his body produced. Today, even middle-class people the world over are living lives that are contributing to great environmental destruction, by consuming things that we may not need and things that may not even be good for us. Perhaps all of us should have chamber pots containing our old cell phones and televisions, as well as samples from lagoons of hog waste—in short, a sampling of the waste products that our middle-class lives produce. If we spent more time examining and reflecting upon our waste, we might become better stewards of the earth's precious resources.

There is abundant evidence that global warming is occurring and that those of us who drive cars, eat meat, and use air conditioners contribute to it. Granted, our understanding of global warming is evolving, but there are good reasons to suspect that the poor will suffer the most. They are the ones who are most susceptible to interruptions in food and water supplies. They are the ones most likely to die in floods or live next to and suffer from lagoons of waste. The wealthy pollute and the poor suffer the consequences of that pollution. To the extent that we live lives of affluence—drive cars, use air conditioning and eat meat—we are using more than our share of the global sink, and for many of us, it will not be easy to change. History is full of people who have tried to escape moral responsibility by claiming not to see what was going on around them. Such appeals to ignorance are rarely persuasive, and in the case of global warming, they are no longer credible. But if concern for others does not persuade us, then consider the unpleasant thought of living in a world made unstable by persistent disruptions in food supplies. We might also think about how we are going to explain our wasteful ways to our grandchildren.

NOTES

Parts of chapter 4 greatly expand upon an article published in *Toward Greater Human Solidarity: Options for a Plural World*, edited by Anindita N. Balslev (Kolkata: Dasgupta &Co. , 2005).

1. Desmond Tutu "Africa—Up in Smoke? The Second Report from the Working Group on Climate Change and Development" http://panos.org.uk/wp-content/files/2011/03/Up_in_smoke_Africa1Odenlf.pdf

2. For a good collection of essays dealing with the ethics of contemporary environmental issues see *Climate Ethics: Essential Readings* ed. Stephen Gardiner (Oxford: Oxford University Press, 2010).

3. See the United Nations report http://unfccc.int/essential_background/feeling_the_heat/items/2904.php

4. See "A Report of Working Group I of the Intergovernmental Panel on Climate Change." The information I just cited comes from the "Summary for Policymakers."

5. Peter Schwartz and Doug Randall, *An Abrupt Climate Change Scenario and Its Implications for United States National Security* (Emeryville, CA: Global Business Network, 2003). See also: *Guardian Unlimited* "Now the Pentagon tells Bush climate change will destroy us" 2/22/04.

6. *An Abrupt Climate Change Scenario and Its Implications for the United States National Security* as quoted in *State of the World 2005* (Washington DC: Norton, 2005) For a more recent report on the scientific consensus when it comes to climate change see http://www.skepticalscience.com/global-warming-scientific-consensus-intermediate.htm. This website lists in exhaustive detail the scientific organizations that have officially stated that climate change is real and is being caused by human activity. It also gives the breakdown on articles published in peer-reviewed publications and cites the study that showed 97 percent of the published papers on climate change (in peer-reviewed journals) that took a stand on the issue argued that human activity was the cause of climate change.

7. *State of the World* 2005 p. 72.

8. *State of the World 2005* p. 72.

9. "Africa—Up in Smoke?

10. These remarks were quoted in the *Guardian Unlimited* "One in Six Countries Facing Food Shortage" 6/30/05.

11. Ibid.

12. http://unfccc.int/essential_background/feeling_the_heat/items/2904.php

13. *One World,* 18. See also "Africa—Up in Smoke?" p. 30. For stories that bring home what this means on individual lives see: http://www.theguardian.com/environment/2009/aug/21/climate-change-nile-flooding-farming

14. *Vital Signs* 88.

15. *New York Times* 12/15/2004.

16. Singer *One World* 21.

17. *Vital Signs* p. 40.

18. "The Fridge, the Greenhouse and the Carbon Sink" *New Internationalist* issue 230, April 1992. http://www.newint.org/issue230/fridge.htm. I first learned about article from reading Singer's *How Are We to Live: Ethics in an Age of Self-Interest* p. 46-7.

19. http://siteresources.worldbank.org/EXTNEWSCHINESE/Resources/3196537-1202098669693/EV_Report_en.pdf

20. "Capitalist Roaders" *New York Times* 7/2/06.

21. http://chinaautoweb.com/2011/03/update-how-many-cars-are-there-in-china/

22. http://www.rediff.com/money/2004/oct/23car.htm

23. Paul Harris also argues that we should recognize that there are differences within countries and that we should not let those who are heavy contributors to climate change off the hook merely because they live in a poor or developing country. "Climate Change and Global Citizenship." *Law & Policy*, Vol. 30, No. 4, pp. 481-501, October 2008

24. Jose Goldemberg et al, *Energy for a Sustainable World*, Worldwatch Institue, Washington, DC 1987, cited by Singer in *How Are We To Live* p. 49.

25. Richard W. Miller *Globalizing Justice* (Oxford UK: Oxford University Press, 2010) p. 98.

26. http://green.blogs.nytimes.com/2011/04/11/awards-season-for-environmentalists/?scp=1&sq=germany%20goldman%20prize&st=cse

27. http://topics.nytimes.com/top/news/business/energy-environment/wind-power/index.html

28. Ibid. p. 37.

29. Howard Frumkin, Lawrence Frank, Richard Jackson *Urban Sprawl and Public Health: Designing, Planning, and Building for Healthy Communities* (Washington: Island Press, 2004) p. xiii.

30. Ibid.

31. Ibid. p. xi.

32. Wernette D.R., Nieves L.A., "Breathing polluted air; Minorities are disproportionately exposed." *EPA Journal* 1992; 18:16-17. As quoted in *Urban Sprawl and Public Health* p. 273 n. 89.

33. *Urban Sprawl and Public Health* p. 199.

34. Peter Singer and Jim Mason, *The Ethics of What We Eat* 146-147. For the study of tomatoes in the UK see: Alison Smith et al, *The Validity of Food Miles as an Indicator of Sustainable Development*, ED50254, Issue 7, July 2005, p. 67; For the study on Swedish agriculture see: A. Carlson, Greenhouse Gas Emissions in the Life-Cycle of Carrots and Tomatoes: methods, data, and results. Environmental and Energy Systems Studies, Lund University, Sweden, March 1997.

35. See Singer, *How Are We to Live*, Prometheus Books, 1995 pages 44-45.

36. http://www.epa.gov/rlep/faq.html

37. "Nitrous Oxide from Agricultural Sources: Potential Role in Greenhouse Gas Emission Reduction and Ozone Recovery," Kelsi Bracmort, Congressional Research Service, 7-5700, www.crs.gov

38. Henning Steinfeld et al. *Livestock's Long Shadow: Environmental Issues and Options* (Food and Agricultural Organization of the United Nations: Rome, 2006). This report can be found online: ftp://ftp.fao.org/docrep/fao/010/A0701E/A0701E00.pdf

39. "Red Meat Production in Australia: Life Cycle Assessment and Comparison with Overseas Studies" *Environ. Sci. Technol.*, 2010, *44* (4), pp 1327–1332.

40. See Maurice E. Pitesky, Kimberly R. Stackhouse, and Frank M. Mitloehner, "Clearing the Air: Livestock's Contribution to Climate Change." In Donald Sparks, editor: *Advances in Agronomy*, Vol. 103, Burlington: Academic Press, 2009, pp. 1-40. Also found at http://animalscience.ucdavis.edu/faculty/mitloehner/publications/2009%20pitesky%20Clearing%20the%20Air.pdf

41. See the executive summary of the EPA's report at http://www.epa.gov/climatechange/emissions/downloads11/US-GHG-Inventory-2011-Executive-Summary.pdf

42. "In Brazil, Paying Farmers to Let the Trees Stand" *New York Times* 9/21/09.

43. "Deforestation Slows as Brazil Chugs Towards a Goal" *New York Times* 12/2/10.

44. Maurice E. Pitesky, Kimberly R. Stackhouse, and Frank M. Mitloehner, "Clearing the Air: Livestock's Contribution to Climate Change." p. 28

45. http://www.extension.org/pages/35850/on-average-how-many-pounds-of-corn-make-one-pound-of-beef-assuming-an-all-grain-diet-from-background

46. Amartya Sen *Development as Freedom* (New York: Anchor Books, 1999) p. 205-6.

47. Quoted in *The Food Revolution* p. 267.

48. Ibid. p. 268.

49. Reijnders, L., and S. Soret, 2003: "Quantification of the environmental impact of different dietary protein choices." *Amer. J. Clin. Nutr.*, 78 (Suppl.), 664S–668S.

50. Christopher L. Weber and H. Scott Matthews, "Food Miles and the Relative Climate Impacts of Food choices in the United States," *Environmental Technology and Science* 2008, 42 3508-3513.

51. http://agcompetitiveness.blogspot.com/2011/04/more-food-for-thought.html

52. For a recent study of aquifer depletion see McGuire, V.L., 2009, Water-level changes in the High Plains aquifer, predevelopment to 2007, 2005–06, and 2006–07: U.S. Geological Survey Scientific Investigations Report 2009–5019, 9 p., available at: http://pubs.usgs.gov/sir/2009/5019/.

53. "US Farmers Fear the Return of Dust Bowl" *The Telegraph* 3/7/2011.

54. Groundwater Depletion Raises Likelihood of Global Food Crises *National Geographic* 9/27/2010

55. http://www.ewg.org/losingground/report

56. Paul Krugman "Economists go for the green" *Slate* 4/18/1997

57. U.S. General Accounting Office, Briefing Report to the Committee on Agriculture, Nutrition and Forestry, U.S. Senate, "Animal Agriculture, Information on Waste Management and Water Quality Issues," GAO/RCED 95-200BR, Washington, DC, pp. 58-61.

58. "Abortions Possibly Related to Ingestion of Nitrate-Contaminated Well Water La-Grange County, Indiana 1991-1994," Morbidity and Mortality Report, Report 26, Centers for Disease Control (July 5, 1996), pp 569-571.

59. R.L. Huffman and P.W. Westerman, "Estimated Seepage Losses from Established Swine Waste Lagoons in the Lower Coastal Plain in North Carolina," transactions of the ASAE 38(2):449-453 (1995).

60. Steve Wing and Susanne Wolf "Intensive Livestock Operations, Health, and Quality of Life among Eastern North Carolina Residents" *Environmental Health Perspectives* vol. 108, no. 3, March 2000 pp.233-237.

61. *Vital Signs* p. 24.

62. Michael de Montaigne *The Complete Essays of Montaigne* trans. Donald Frame (Stanford: Stanford University Press, 1965) p. 721.

63. I am getting this definition of hazardous waste as well as many other points in this section from Ruchi Anand's *International Environmental Justice: A North-South Dimension* (Burlington, VT: Ashgate, 2004) p. 61.

64. Zada Lipman "A Dirty Dilemma: The Hazardous Waste Trade" *Harvard International Review* vol. 23, no. 4, Winter 2002.

65. Lipman

66. http://www.epa.gov/compliance/resources/publications/monitoring/programs/importexport/trade.pdf

67. Ibid. p. 66

68. http://www.ban.org/ban_news/2011/110413_cea_new_initiative.html

Conclusion

Wealth in and of itself is not problematic. If some were wealthy while everyone had the basics—food, shelter, health care, and leisure time—then inequality would not be such a bad thing. Many people who have it will tell you that there are many things money can't buy. But today we live in a world where many are wealthy and many are desperately poor. In this world of savage inequalities many lack drinking water, food, clothes, shoes, a safe place to go to the bathroom, and a roof over their heads. Moreover, the world is wealthy enough right now to reduce significantly or even eliminate the worst poverty. Inequalities are savage when some lack water, food and shelter while others have garages with thirty-six Porsches, yachts that cost $200 million to build and $20 million a year to maintain, or a twenty-seven-story house in Mumbai.

Not having the wealth of Jerry Seinfield, Paul Allen, or Mukesh Ambani, I am not poor. If we stop to consider the masses that live on less than $2.00 a day, many of us will have to concede that we are relatively wealthy. Even in the United States, there are many who are poor compared to me. I do not have to know exactly what justice is to know that something should be done about the inequalities of our age. How can I have so much when so many have so little? I have worked hard at times in my life, but many of the poor work much harder. I am very fortunate to have been born to middle-class parents in the wealthiest nation in the world and to have been born without any serious disabilities. Given my luck, I can give some of my money to support effective charitable organizations and use some of the political freedom that I enjoy to lobby so that the poor might be fairly compensated for their labor and the minerals that very often are found in the ground beneath their feet. Given my luck, I should try to do something for those who were not born with such luck. I also need to do something about my contributions

111

to global warming that threatens many of the world's most vulnerable people. There is nothing wrong with charity, but given the ways that even middle-class lives are at least in part purchased at great cost to the poor the world over, we owe more than charity. We consume valuable resources when we drive our cars and cool and heat our homes. The rare earth metals in our phones and computers lead to suffering in China and Africa. Even middle-class life rests on the exploitation of the poor, so we owe restitution and not just charity to the poor.

Aristotle is right that no two ethical situations are ever the same and that we can never be sure how our actions will turn out. Ethics is an imprecise endeavor. I cannot say exactly what anyone should do about the poverty in the world. Everyone's situation is different, but we should not let the uncertainty of ethics deter all action. No reason to be a dithering Hamlet. The poor need help and they need justice and there are many steps that can be taken right away and will not demand much in the way of sacrifice. No reason to be Aristophanes' Socrates, lost in the clouds of theory philosophizing while peering into the ass of a flea. Many of the ethical decisions we need to make are not that complex. How many persons concerned about global warming does it take to change an incandescent light bulb and replace it with an LED bulb. No reason to be a martyr—the track record of crusading reformers and martyrs leaves much to be desired. Start by overcoming the lethargy that often accompanies bourgeois life. Start by picking the low-lying fruit. Eat less meat, drive less, walk—you will be healthier and it should save you money as well. Take some action and attempt to make the political system more just.

It is easy to ignore the poverty of this world, but we should resist the temptation to do so. Recognize privilege, something that is all too easy to overlook. If we have a roof over our heads, food, health care, clean water to drink, and leisure time we are doing better than most of the world. Recognize that the accident of birth has a great deal to do with where we end up. Once we become a member of the wealthy, there are numerous systemic advantages that help to keep us wealthy. Think about how we can balance the playing field. How can we insure that all children are given a good education and a real chance to succeed? Think about how we can insure that those who are helping to make our lives possible receive living wages. Who is cleaning our office, or growing, harvesting, and shipping our food? Who is washing the dishes in our favorite restaurant? What can we do to help them receive living wages? Are there merchants in our area that pay living wages and provide health care for their workers? If we can afford to shop at them—why not? Why not buy fair trade products if they are available and we can afford them? The world is, in many ways, a very small place. My laptop and cell phone required, among other things, the labor of a tin miner in the Congo. My car has certainly, at times, been fueled by oil that came from very poor sections of Nigeria and Angola. What have I done for these people? More importantly, what can I do these people?

Particularly for those of us in the United States, our use of the environment is ethically problematic and will take real effort and sacrifice to change. Still some things are easy—energy-efficient light bulbs will save money in the long run. For those of us who can afford them, as cars need to be replaced, fuel-efficiency should be of paramount importance. Fuel efficient cars will also save us money. Save money by turning up our thermostats in the summer and by turning down our heat in the winter. Take public transportation, or if it is not an option, speak out in favor of public transportation. Carpool, ride a bike, or walk whenever possible. Reduce demand for fossil fuel and conserve precious soil and water by eating less meat. To the extent that we eat less meat, take public transportation, walk or ride bikes, we will likely be healthier. Car pools will give us opportunities to spend time with others and get to know them. I don't know anyone who enjoys being stuck in a traffic jam. Let us think of ways to get cars off the road and get more exercise as well as help small farmers in Africa and Asia who rely on seasonal rains and are therefore most vulnerable to erratic weather brought on by global warming.

I don't know how we change the political and economic systems so that everyone in the world earns a living wage and has access to health care, education, and leisure time. I do not know what perfect justice would be, but as a philosopher I can work to increase awareness of the ethical imperative to work toward the eradication of the world's worst poverty. I can join with people who know more about the economic issues and development issues, and they can help us all understand which poverty eradication strategies are most likely to work. We can all listen to and work with the poor who need to be full partners in the eradication efforts. The eradication of poverty will also require experts who understand how the political process works as well as experts who have studied development. We should recognize that concern for poverty often cuts across traditional political lines and form principled coalitions to advance legislation that funds free high-quality public education and health care, and reduces subsidies that unfairly disadvantage small farmers worldwide. We should lobby our governments to improve the plight of the poor at home and abroad. There is much to be learned about how to make this world better. Individuals, NGOs and governments are going to have to try a number of things and see what works. Lend our ideas and our energy to making this world a better place. Working with others to make the world a better place by building coalitions may actually be more fun than going to the mall or shopping by ourselves online. It also holds out the promise of making our world a safer place.

Problems are much easier to see than correct. Well intentioned efforts by smart people sometimes produce bad results. That said, the world has seen much progress in poverty reduction. Working together with the poor we should seek out solutions and rigorously analyze our efforts to reduce poverty. As I write this, there are reports of infant and maternal deaths being averted in Liberia thanks to a $35 million program that eliminates all hospital fees for pregnant women. A vaccine that offers some protection against malaria has been developed. Many countries have shown that poverty can be greatly reduced if smart investments are made in the right programs. *The Economist* reports that over the first ten years of this century, six of the world's ten fastest-growing economies are in sub-Saharan Africa. In the next decade, they predict that seven out of ten will be in this region.[1] Angola, Nigeria, and Equatorial Guinea are very wealthy countries. If we join with activists in those countries to help spread wealth more justly we would not only help to reduce poverty, but we would also reduce pressure in wealthy countries to cut deals with shady characters. Bringing justice to those who live in mineral-rich states, helps make wealthy first world nations more just as well. The world is increasingly interconnected. Injustice anywhere is truly a threat to justice everywhere. Working to reduce poverty may also be one of the most satisfying things a human can do.

NOTES

1. *The Economist,* "Africa's Impressive Growth," 6 January 2011.

Bibliography

Agarwal, Anil and Sunita Narain. "The Fridge, the Greenhouse and the Carbon Sink" *New Internationalist* issue 230, April 1992.

Anand, Ruchi. *International Environmental Justice: A North-South Dimension* (Burlington, VT: Ashgate, 2004).

Aristotle. *The Politics and the Constitution of Athens* trans. Jowett, revised (New York: Cambridge University Press, 1996).

———. *Nicomachean Ethics* trans. Terence Irwin (Indianapolis: Hackett Publishing Company, 1999).

Ashford, Elizabeth. "The Alleged Dichotomy between Positive and Negative Rights and Duties" in Charles R. Beitz and Robert E. Goodin, eds. *Global Basic Rights* (Oxford UK: Oxford University Press, 2009) pp. 92-112.

BanerjeeAbhijit, Banerjeeand Esther Duflo. *Poor Economics: A Radical Rethinking of the Way to Fight Global Poverty* (Washington, DC: Public Affairs, 2011).

Baradaran, Shima and Barclay, Stephanie H., "Fair Trade and Child Labor" *Columbia Human Rights Law Review*, 4/26/2011.

Berlin, Isaiah. "Two Concepts of Liberty" in *Liberty: Incorporating Four Essays on Liberty* ed. Henry Hardy 2ed. (Oxford: Oxford, 2002).

Beitz, Charles. "Justice and International Relations" in *International Ethics* ed. Beitz, Cohen, Scalon and Simmons (Princeton: Princeton University Press, 1985).

Bush, George W. Untitled (Speech announcing the beginning of military actions in Iraq) given on March 19, 2003. Found at "President Bush's Address on the Iraq Invasion," *Wall Street Journal* http://blogs.wsj.com/dispatch/2013/03/18/full-text-of-president-george-w-bushs-speech-march-19-2003/

Bracmort, Kelsi. "Nitrous Oxide from Agricultural Sources: Potential Role in Greenhouse Gas Emission Reduction and Ozone Recovery," Congressional Research Service, 7-5700, www.crs.gov.

Calderisi, Robert. *The Trouble with Africa: Why Foreign Aid Isn't Working* (New York: Palgrave, 2006).

Ci, Jiwei. "What Negative Duties? Which Moral Universalism?" In *Thomas Pogge and His Critics* (Cambridge: Polity, 2010).

Cline, William, R. *Trade Policy and Global Poverty* (Washington, DC: Center for Global Development, 2004).

Cohen, Joshua. "Philosophy, Social Science and Global Poverty" in *Thomas Pogge and His Critics* ed. Alison Jaggar (Cambridge UK: Polity, 2010) pp. 18-45.

Collier, Paul. *The Bottom Billion* (Oxford: Oxford University Press, 2008)

Collins, Patricia Hill *Black Feminist Thought* 2nd ed. (New York: Routledge, 2008).

Fernandez de Córdoba, Santiago and David Vanzetti, "Now What? Searching for a Solution to the WTO Industrial Tariff Negotiations," in Sam Laird and Santiago Fernandez de Córdoba (eds), *Coping with Trade Reforms: A Developing-Country Perspective on the WTO Industrial Tariff Negotiations* (Basingstoke: Palgrave Macmillan, 2006).

Cullity, Garrett. *The Moral Demands of Affluence* (Oxford: Clarendon Press, Oxford University Press, 2004).

Easterly, William. *White Man's Burden: Why the West's Efforts to Aid the Rest Have Done So Much Ill and So Little Good* (New York: Penguin 2006).

Edmonds, Eric V. "Does Child Labor Decline with Improving Economic Status?" *Journal of Human Resources*, vol. 40 no. 1, 2005.

——"The Effect of Trade Liberalization on Child Labor" *Journal of International Economics* 2005.

Ehrenreich, Barbara. *Nickeled and Dimed: On Not Getting By in America* (Holt: New York, 2007).

Elfenbein, Daniel W. and Brian McManus. "A Greater Price for a Greater Good? Evidence that Consumers Pay More for Charity-Linked Products" *American Economic Journal: Economic Policy*, vol. 2, no. 2, 2010 pp. 28-60.

Fischer, Stanley. *IMF Essays from a Time of Crisis: The International Financial System, Stabilization, and Development* (Cambridge: The MIT Press, 2004).

Frumkin, Howard, Lawrence, Frank, and Richard Jackson. *Urban Sprawl and Public Health: Designing, Planning, and Building for Healthy Communities* (Washington, DC: Island Press, 2004).

Gardiner, Stephen ed. *Climate Ethics: Essential Readings* (Oxford: Oxford University Press, 2010).

Ghazvinian, John. *Untapped: The Scramble for Africa's Oil* (Orlando: Harcourt, 2007).

Goldemberg, Jose et al, *Energy for a Sustainable World*, Worldwatch Institute, Washington, DC 1987.

Harris, Paul. Climate Change and Global Citizenship. *Law & Policy*, Vol. 30, No. 4, pp. 481-501, October 2008.

Huffman R.L. and P.W. Westerman, "Estimated Seepage Losses from Established Swine Waste Lagoons in the Lower Coastal Plain in North Carolina," transactions of the ASAE 38(2):449-453 (1995).

Humphreys, Macartan, Jeffrey D. Sachs, and Joseph Stiglitz, eds., *Escaping the Resource Curse* (New York: Columbia University Press, 2007).

Jaggar, Alison M. ed. *Thomas Pogge and His Critics* (Cambridge: Polity, 2010).

Jones, Charles *Global Justice: Defending Cosmopolitanism* (Oxford UK: Oxford University Press, 1999).

Johnston, David Cay. *Perfectly Legal: The Covert Campaign to Rig Our Tax System to Benefit the Super Rich—And Cheat Everybody Else* (New York: Portfolio, 2003).

Kozol, Jonathan *Savage Inequalities* (New York: HarperPerennial, 1991).

—— *Shame of the Nation* (New York: Crown Publishers, 2005).

Krugman, Paul. "In Praise of Cheap Labor: Bad jobs are better than no jobs at all." *Slate* 3/20/97.

—— "Economists go for the Green" *Slate* 4/18/1997.

—— "Saving Asia, it is Time to get Radical" (*Fortune* Magazine 9/7/98).

Kuper, Andrew. "Global Poverty Relief: More than Charity" in *Global Responsibilities: Who Must Deliver on Human Rights* ed. (New York: Routledge, 2005).

Lorde, Audre. "Uses of the Erotic: The Erotic as Power" *Sister Outsider: Essays and Speeches*. (Freedom, CA: Crossing Press, 1984).

Lipman, Zada. "A Dirty Dilemma: The Hazardous Waste Trade" *Harvard International Review* vol.23 no 4 winter 2002.

Maas, Peter. *Crude World: The Violent Twilight of Oil* (Vintage: New York, 2009).

Marx, Karl. "Theses on Feuerbach" https://www.marxists.org/archive/marx/works/1845/theses/theses.htm

Mattioli, Maria C. and V.K. Sapovadia, "Laws of Labor: Core Labor Standards and Global Trade" *Harvard International Review* vol. xxvi, no. 2, summer 2004.

Milanovic, Branko. "Where in the Global Income Distribution Are You?" in *The Haves and Have-Nots: A Brief and Idiosyncratic History of Global Inequality* (New York: Basic, 2011).

Mill, John Stewart. *Utilitarianism* (Indianapolis: Hackett, 2002).

Miller, Richard W. *Globalizing Justice: The Ethics of Poverty and Power* (Oxford: Oxford University Press, 2010).

Mills, Charles W. "Realizing (Through Racializing) Pogge" in *Thomas Pogge and His Critics.* pp 151-174.

Mitloehner, Frank. "Red Meat Production in Australia: Life Cycle Assessment and Comparison with Overseas Studies" *Environ. Sci. Technol.*, 2010, *44* (4), pp 1327–1332.

Montaigne, Michael de. *The Complete Essays of Montaigne* trans. Donald Frame (Stanford: Stanford University Press, 1965).

Munk, Nina. *The Idealist* (New York: Doubleday, 2013).

Nielson, Kai *Globalization and Justice* (Amherst, New York: Humanity Books, 2003).

Nietzsche, Friedrich. *Dawn: Thoughts on the Prejudices of Philosophy,* (Berlin: dtv deGruyter 1980).

——*Beyond Good and Evil: Prelude to a Philosophy of the Future* (Berlin: dtv deGruyter 1980).

——*On the Genealogy of Morals:* (Berlin: dtv deGruyter 1980).

Noah, Timothy. "The United States of Inequality" *Slate* 9/3/2010 http://www.slate.com/id/2266025/entry/2266816/

Nussbaum, Martha. *Sex and Social Justice* (New York: Oxford University Press, 1999).

O'Neill, Onora. *Bounds of Justice* (Cambridge UK: Cambridge University Press, 2000).

Pitesky, Maurice E., Kimberly R. Stackhouse, and Frank M. Mitloehner, "Clearing the Air: Livestock's Contribution to Climate Change" In Donald Sparks, editor: *Advances in Agronomy*, Vol. 103, Burlington: Academic Press, 2009, pp. 1-40. Also found athttp://animalscience.ucdavis.edu/faculty/mitloehner/publications/2009%20pitesky%20Clearing%20the%20Air.pdf

Plato. *Theaetetus* trans. Seth Benardete (Chicago: The University of Chicago Press, 1986).

Pogge, Thomas. *World Development and Human Rights* (Cambridge, UK: Polity, 2002).

—— "Assisting the Global Poor" in *The Ethics of Assistance* ed. Deen K. Chatterjee (Cambridge: Cambridge University Press, 2007. pp. 260-288.

——*Politics as Usual* (Cambridge, UK: Polity 2009).

Pogge, Thomas, ed. *Global Justice* (Oxford, UK: Blackwell, 2001).

——*Global Institutions and Responsibilities: Achieving Global Justice* (Malden MA: Blackwell, 2005).

Rawls, John. *A Theory of Justice* (Cambridge: Harvard University Press, 1971).

——*The Law of Peoples* (Cambridge: Harvard University Press, 2001).

Reijnders, L., and S. Soret, 2003: "Quantification of the environmental impact of different dietary protein choices." *Amer. J. Clin. Nutr.*, 78 (Suppl.), 664S–668S.

Reinikka, Ritva and Svensson, Jakob, "Local Capture and the Political Economy of School Financing," *Quarterly Journal of Economics* 119 (2004), pp. 679-705.

Rivoli, Pietra. *Travels of a T-Shirt in the Global Economy: An Economist Examines the Markets, Power, and Politics of the World* (Wiley, New York, 2005).

Sachs, Jeffrey. *The End of Poverty* (Penguin: New York, 2006).

Sandel, Michael. *Justice: What Is the Right Thing to Do?* (New York: Farrar, Straus and Giroux).

Schopenhauer, Arthur. *The World As Will and Representation* trans. E.F.J. Payne (Mineola: Dover, 1966).

Schwartz, David T. *Consuming Choices: Ethics in a Global Consumer World* (Lanham: Rowman & Littlefield, 2010).

Schwartz, Peter and Randall, Doug. *An Abrupt Climate Change Scenario and Its Implications for United States National Security* (Emeryville, CA. Global Business Network, 2003).

Shaxson, Nicholas. *The Dirty Politics of African Oil* (Pelgrave: New York, 2007),

Sen, Amartya *Development as Freedom* (Oxford: Oxford University Press, 1999).
———*The Idea of Justice*, (Cambridge: Harvard University Press, 2009).
——— (with Jean Dreze) *An Uncertain Glory: India and its Contradictions* (Princeton NJ: Princeton University Press, 2013).
Shaefer, H. Luke, and Edin, Kathryn. "Rising Extreme Poverty in the United States and the Response of Federal Means-Tested Programs" National Poverty Center Working Paper Series #13-06, May 2013.
Shue, Henry. *Basic Rights: Subsistence, Affluence, and U.S. Foreign Policy* 2nd ed. (Princeton: Princeton University Press, 1996).
Singer, Peter. "Famine, Affluence and Morality" *Philosophy and Public Affairs* 1, no. 3 (Spring 1972).
———*Practical Ethics* (Cambridge: Cambridge University Press, 1993).
——— *How Are We to Live: Ethics in an Age of Self Interest* (Amherst, NY: Prometheus Books, 1995).
———*Ethics into Action: Henry Spira and the Animal Rights Movement* (Lanham MD: Rowman & Littlefield, 2000).
———*One World* (New Haven: Yale University Press, 2002).
———*President of Good and Evil: Questioning the Ethics of George W. Bush* (New York: Plume, 2004).
———with Jim Mason, *The Ethics of What We Eat* (Rodale, 2006).
———*The Life You Can Save* (New York: Random House, 2009).
Smith, Alison. et al, *The Validity of Food Miles as an Indicator of Sustainable Development*, ED50254, Issue 7, July 2005.
Stiglitz, Joseph. *Globalization and Its Discontents* (New York: Norton, 2003).
———. and Andrew Charlton, *Fair Trade for All: How Trade Can Promote Development* (Oxford: Oxford University Press, 2005).
———. *Making Globalization Work.* (New York: Norton, 2006).
Steinfeld, Henning, et al. *Livestock's Long Shadow: Environmental Issues and Options* (Food and Agricultural Organization of the United Nations: Rome, 2006). This report can be found online: ftp://ftp.fao.org/docrep/fao/010/A0701E/A0701E00.pdf
Tutu, Desmond. Foreword to "Africa—Up in Smoke? The Second Report from the Working Group on Climate Change and Development" http://panos.org.uk/wp-content/files/2011/03/Up_in_smoke_Africa1Odenlf.pdf
Twining, Dan. "An Indian election primer" *Foreign Policy,* 4/16/2009.
Vizard, Polly, *Poverty and Human Rights: Sen's 'Capability Perspective' Explored* (Oxford: Oxford University Press, 2006).
Weber, Christopher L. and H. Scott Matthews. "Food Miles and the Relative Climate Impacts of Food Choices in the United States," *Environmental Technology and Science* 2008, 42. pp. 3508-3513.
Wenar, Leif. "Poverty Is No Pond", in Patricia Illingworth, Thomas Pogge and Leif Wenar, eds, *Giving Well: The Ethics of Philanthropy* (Oxford: Oxford University Press, 2011).
West, Cornel. *Race Matters* (New York: Vintage Books, 1994).
Wang, Feng and Xuejin Zuo. "Inside China's Cities: Institutional Barriers and Opportunities for Urban Migrants. " *American Economic Review* 89, no. 2, 1999, pp. 276-280.
Wernette D.R., Nieves L.A. "Breathing Polluted Air; Minorities are disproportionately exposed." *EPA Journal* 1992; 18:16-17.
Wing, Steve and Wolf, Susanne. "Intensive Livestock Operations, Health, and Quality of Life among Eastern North Carolina Residents" *Environmental Health Perspectives* vol. 108, no. 3 March 2000 pp. 233-237.
Zizek, Slavoj. *The Year of Dreaming Dangerously* (London, Verso, 2012).

Index

CPSIA information can be obtained at www.ICGtesting.com
Printed in the USA
BVOW08*0116140715

408201BV00004B/4/P